D1544245

PORTFOLIO
BEHAVIOR OF
FINANCIAL
INSTITUTIONS

HOLT, RINEHART AND WINSTON SERIES IN FINANCE

William Beranek, Series Editor
Pennsylvania State University

Joseph F. Bradley
ADMINISTRATIVE FINANCIAL MANAGEMENT, Second Edition
Adolph E. Grunewald and Erwin E. Nemmers
BASIC MANAGERIAL FINANCE
Paul F. Jessup
INNOVATIONS IN BANK MANAGEMENT: Selected Readings
Glen A. Mumey
THEORY OF FINANCIAL STRUCTURE
David Novick
PROGRAM BUDGETING, Second Edition
Alexander A. Robichek and Alan B. Coleman
MANAGEMENT OF FINANCIAL INSTITUTIONS: Notes and Cases
William L. Silber
PORTFOLIO BEHAVIOR OF FINANCIAL INSTITUTIONS
Donald Vaughn
SURVEY OF INVESTMENTS
J. Fred Weston and Eugene F. Brigham
ESSENTIALS OF MANAGERIAL FINANCE
Leland Yeager
THE INTERNATIONAL MONETARY MECHANISM

Forthcoming Titles

William Beranek
CAPITAL BUDGETING THEORY
Eugene F. Brigham and Steven Hawk
CASES IN FINANCE
Eugene F. Brigham and Keith Smith
CAPITAL BUDGETING
William H. Jean
ANALYTICAL THEORY OF FINANCE
G. D. Quirin
INVESTMENT ANALYSIS

PORTFOLIO BEHAVIOR OF FINANCIAL INSTITUTIONS

An Empirical Study with Implications
for Monetary Policy, Interest-Rate
Determination, and Financial Model-Building

WILLIAM L. SILBER

Associate Professor of Economics
Graduate School of Business
New York University

HOLT, RINEHART AND WINSTON, INC.
New York   Chicago   San Francisco   Atlanta
Dallas   Montreal   Toronto   London   Sydney

To my parents
Joseph F. and Pauline R. Silber (s'lta)

FOREWORD

In preparing and writing this manuscript, I have benefited from the help of numerous individuals. My greatest intellectual debt goes to Stephen M. Goldfeld and Lester V. Chandler, who guided an earlier version of this study. To my teachers in stabilization policy, econometrics, and monetary economics—Richard Musgrave, Richard Quandt, and Edward J. Kane, respectively—I owe special thanks for imparting an analytical approach to real-world problems. Burton Malkiel provided important technical information. My research assistant, Charles Tapiero, performed diligently, above and beyond the call of duty. The regression program used in estimating the equations of the model was constructed by Peter Tinsley. I owe him many thanks because the unique features of his program were invaluable. Lee Silman is to be commended for her excellent typing of a difficult manuscript. The Federal Deposit Insurance Corporation, which provided funds for work on another project, also deserves my gratitude because that work and this manuscript are interrelated. Above all, special thanks are due my wife, Lillian, for her willingness to bear with the unbearable during the final stages of this project—and most importantly, to do so with a smile. She also helped in the preparation of the tables in Chapter 5. Finally, Jonathan Mark was of great help since he left his daddy's papers unscribbled upon—usually.

TECHNICAL NOTE: The equations presented in this book are centered on the page (rather than lined up on the left-hand margin) for easier integration with the text.

New York, New York   W. L. S.
October 1969

CONTENTS

TABLES

PORTFOLIO
BEHAVIOR OF
FINANCIAL
INSTITUTIONS

Chapter 1

INTRODUCTORY REMARKS

INTRODUCTION

The financial sector of the economy fulfills an extremely important function, namely, the allocation of capital among alternative uses. In addition, the efficiency of the financial sector influences the overall consumption-versus-saving decision of the public. The importance of the money and capital markets in a free enterprise economy is, therefore, beyond dispute. A full understanding of the workings of these markets and the institutions that operate in them is essential to any serious student of monetary and financial economics.

There are a number of provocative issues that have long been subject to discussion by economists interested in monetary problems. The series of studies prepared for the Commission on Money and Credit (CMC) is but one example of the voluminous literature devoted to an analysis of at least the following three important issues in monetary economics: (1) the effectiveness of monetary policy,[1] (2) the general behavior of financial institutions in the capital markets,[2] and (3) the role that financial intermediaries play in the allocation of capital in the financial markets.[3]

There is one common thread connecting these three issues, that is, the degree to which different categories of securities are substitutes for one another in lender portfolios. One of the objectives of this study is to shed some light on this very question and to analyze the implications forthcoming for monetary policy and capital allocation. An attempt will be made also to describe the general portfolio behavior of the major financial intermediaries currently prominent in the U.S. financial structure. The impact of stabilization policy on financial institution portfolio behavior shall also be explored. This is one area that most recent econometric models (even those interested in the financial sector) have ignored.

In order to examine these and other questions of related interest, a quarterly econometric model of the U.S. economy with major emphasis on portfolio behavior of financial institutions will be estimated. The Federal Reserve Board's Flow of Funds Accounts provides the framework for the model. A brief description of the structural system and the reduced form is set forth in the next section of this chapter. Further discussion of the importance of portfolio substitutability between securities now follows.

The hypothesis that different categories of securities (for example, Government bonds, corporate bonds, municipals, and mortgages) are good substitutes for one another in lender portfolios is extremely important for the proponents of the position that monetary policy is an effective stabilization weapon. Assume, for example, that the Federal Reserve System ("Fed") wishes to implement a tight monetary policy. There are a number of linkages between the policy variables controlled by the "Fed" and the final objective in this case, that is, total spending. Using open market operations, its basic tool, the monetary authority can sell Government securities in the open market in order to bring about a tightening of credit to the private sector of the economy. Although there are many aspects to a "tightening of credit," such as, perhaps, the degree of credit rationing, the major traditional indicator of the efficacy of monetary policy is the level of interest rates. This approach, of course,

---

[1] See [9] and [11]. (In all footnotes, numbers in brackets refer to entry numbers of references at the end of the book.)
[2] See [37], [1] and [40].
[3] For example, see Chapter II in [37] and Chapter 10 in [40].

is within the credit view of the monetary process.[4] The interest rates that ought to be the major concern of monetary policy are the rates attached to the credit instruments of the private sector of the economy. Because the "Fed" can carry out open market operations only with Government securities, it must be assumed, in this simplified example, that somewhere in the economy Government bonds (Governments) and (say) corporate bonds (corporates) are substitutes for one another in investment portfolios. If Governments and corporates were not good substitutes, it is easy to see that the effect of open market operations would not be felt that strongly in the corporate bond market and monetary policy would be a less powerful stabilization weapon.

As far as fiscal and debt policy are concerned, the issue of the substitutability between various securities is important for the following reason. In addition to the fiscal effect of government expenditure there also exists a monetary effect, that is, the impact of the way the expenditure is financed. If the government finances its expenditure through the issue of new money, the monetary effect of the expenditure will definitely be expansionary. If government purchases are financed by issuing more bonds, then the monetary effect of the expenditure will depend upon the substitute-complement relationship between different categories of private and Government securities.[5]

Let us now turn to the relationship between the substitution question and the allocative function of the capital markets. We can say that, in general, capital ought to flow into the areas that have the highest rates of return. Furthermore, this flow of capital should occur with a relatively small inducement via changes in rates of return and relative interest rates. For example, a small increase in the corporate bond rate relative to the mortgage rate should attract funds toward corporate bonds (and corporate investment) and away from mortgage lending (and home building). This flow of funds will be desirable as long as the rate of interest offered on each security bears some relationship to the profitability in each sector. If corporates and mortgages are good substitutes for each other in lender portfolios, perhaps only a slight change in relative yield would be required to effect the desired change in the direction of the flow

---

[4] For a comparison of the money-versus-credit views of the monetary process in this context see [50]. The credit view and in particular the interest-sensitivity-of-investment subcategory stresses the effect of policy on interest rates and the effect of rates on investment spending. The monetary view stresses the direct impact of money supply on spending. Our entire study is within the credit-view framework.

[5] For an excellent discussion, see [8], Research Study Four, "An Essay on Principles of Debt Management" by James Tobin, especially pp. 143–167. A further point is made in [31].

of funds.[6] If the two securities were very poor substitutes (or in the limiting case, were independent in demand), perhaps a huge shift in relative yields would be required to produce the desired result. This would imply that the capital markets are not performing their allocative function in a reasonable way.

It should be noted also that if Government securities are substitutes for some types of private securities, while complementary with others, there exists the possibility of discriminatory effects of monetary and debt policies. This discrimination would present itself both in the final product market and in the financial sector. Under these circumstances a complete reevaluation of these stabilization weapons would be required.

OUTLINE OF THE STUDY

In light of the discussion in the previous section, an empirical test of the hypothesis that different categories of securities are good substitutes for one another in lender portfolios seems to be a worthwhile objective. In this study the hypothesis will be tested with respect to the portfolios of the following financial intermediaries: mutual savings banks, savings and loan associations, commercial banks, pension plans, life insurance companies, and property and casualty insurance companies. Because these intermediaries hold a significantly large proportion of the securities whose interrelationships we would like to ascertain, it is quite probable that we shall be able to make an overall judgment regarding the various substitute-complement relationships.

In order to test the hypothesis, demand equations for each category of security for each financial intermediary will be specified. In each de-

---

[6] In order for capital to be efficiently allocated (in a system without risk) among alternative investment projects, one of two conditions must hold: (1) different categories of securities must be perfect substitutes for one another in the portfolios of financial intermediaries or (2) the liabilities of these institutions must be perfect substitutes for each other in the public's portfolio. These points were made in [16]. Our contention in the text is that condition (1) is extremely important. There is a third condition that, if satisfied, would also insure an efficient allocation of capital, that is, different categories of securities are perfect substitutes for each other in borrower portfolios. Actually, this condition is purely academic because although corporations may be able to issue some (for example) mortgage debt as a substitute for corporate bonds, they cannot issue Government bonds to raise capital.

These conditions do not make any provisions for the possibility of complementarity between the securities. This implies that they are, at best, valid only when complementarity between securities is not reasonable, that is, when there is no risk or uncertainty.

mand equation, the own rate of interest (that is, the rate on the security that is the dependent variable) and rates on alternative assets will appear as explanatory variables, along with other relevant arguments in the demand function. These demand equations will then be estimated by using appropriate statistical techniques. The estimated regression coefficients for the interest rates will be examined and, depending upon the signs (and statistical significance) of the different rates of interest, a conclusion will be forthcoming as to whether there are substitute or complement relationships between the various securities.

The decision to specify the demand equations for each security on a financial institution basis rather than to aggregate across all institutions was made on the grounds that the behavioral relationships may vary considerably from one intermediary to another. An important by-product of the analysis will be a rigorous description of the similarities and differences in the portfolio preferences of financial intermediaries.

The study will be developed in four phases. In Chapter 2 the theoretical underpinnings of the entire analysis will be presented. This discussion will be separated into two parts. In the first section the risk characteristics of different securities will be examined with reference to their possible functions in lender portfolios. This will lay the groundwork for the expected substitute-or-complement relationships between securities. A hypothesis will be formulated regarding the expected relationship between each security in the portfolios of the intermediaries. The second part of this chapter will examine the assumptions underlying the specification of the functional form of the equations to be estimated.

In Chapter 3, the first two sections will contain a discussion of the data to be used in the regression equations, the problems that are involved, and the precise tests that will be used to determine substitutability and complementarity. The rest of the chapter will be devoted to a discussion of the behavioral characteristics of each financial institution and to a presentation of the estimates of the security demand equations.

In Chapter 4 an entire model of economic behavior, with primary emphasis on the financial sector, will be set forth. This model is specified for two main reasons: (1) It is important to recognize the context in which our behavioral equations are operating, as we shall see in Chapter 5 of this study. (2) The use of the two-stage least squares (TSLS) estimating procedure (which is used in all of the estimated equations, except where indicated otherwise) requires a knowledge of the predetermined variables appearing in the other equations of the entire model. We shall then discuss the nature of the model with respect to the determination of all of the endogenous variables. In short, the model consists of eleven financial markets, determining (as endogenous variables) security demands, interest rates on these securities, certain security supplies, the liabilities of three financial intermediaries, the interest rate on time deposits and various items in the market for bank reserves (actually the market for high-powered money, that is, currency plus reserves). In addition, a real sector, consisting of consumption and investment functions and equations defining total, personal, and disposable income, will be appended to the model so that these variables will also be endogenous.

In Chapter 5 we shall analyze the implications of the results for monetary policy, fiscal policy, and capital allocation. The approach will be to calculate the reduced form of the structural system and then to proceed to discuss the implications of the impact multipliers for various policy tools and for capital allocation. A brief discussion will also be presented concerning the differential impacts of various policies on financial intermediary portfolios.

The impact multipliers of open market operations, reserve requirement changes, and discount rate changes will be examined under different assumptions regarding the degree of substitutability between securities in intermediary portfolios. The reduction in the impact multipliers of monetary policy under conditions of reduced degrees of substitutability between securities will be demonstrated clearly. Impact multipliers for exogenous changes in security supplies and/or demands will also be explored under differing degrees of portfolio substitutability. Finally, the strength of monetary policy will be examined through different sets of impact multipliers corresponding to alternative formulations of the structural channels through which monetary policy operates.

Chapter 2

THEORETICAL UNDERPINNINGS

PORTFOLIO RISKS AND SUBSTITUTABILITY

Securities that are candidates for an investor's portfolio can be characterized by two attributes that help determine the ultimate asset composition of the portfolio. The two characteristics are yield and risk. In general, two assets are good substitutes for each other to the extent that they share the same risks. In order to reduce the overall risk of the portfolio, the investment manager diversifies the holdings of securities by including assets that have independent risks. There is a trade-off, naturally, between risk reduction and yield; that is, risk reduction will be sacrificed to some extent under the inducement of higher yield.

There are a number of uncertainties that affect the "risk rating" of various securities. Tobin lists a few that deserve mention here.[1] First, there is the uncertainty about the purchasing power of the dollar. Securities that have a fixed face value in money terms, such as bonds, are subject to this risk. Second, there is uncertainty regarding future interest rates. Capital losses or gains will be made on interest-bearing bonds depending on whether future rates rise or fall. Third, certain securities are tied to very specific assets or to a particular management. Here, the risk of

---

[1] See [8], Research Study Four, pp. 162–167.

default must enter into the portfolio choice. Finally, private equities are subject to the specific risk of uncertainty regarding earning power of a particular firm. There is one other component of risk, not discussed by Tobin, that is closely connected with the secondary market associated with a given security. If two securities are identical in all respects except that one has a well-organized secondary market while the other has a poor secondary market, an investor in the latter runs the risk of being able to liquidate his security holdings only at a depressed price (compared with the price offered for the security with the better market). Factors such as imperfect knowledge on behalf of the participants in the secondary market or the existence of only a small number of traders in the market account for the fact that an attempt to sell a large block of the security requires a significant decrease in price. We shall refer to this characteristic of a security as the marketability risk.

Given these categories of uncertainty, it is possible to contrast the different types of securities to see whether they share similar uncertainties thus making their risk components very similar. Securities which share the same risks are likely to be substitutes. Securities whose risk components are independent may be used to diversify the portfolio. If the risk components of different securities compensate for each other to a great extent, the diversification of the portfolio might actually result in a complementary relationship between these securities; that is, an increase in the yield on security A would increase the demand for security B (at the expense of another group of substitute assets).

As will be discovered in Chapter 3, the substitute-complement relationship beween securities may vary between the different financial intermediaries. Not only is the volatility of liabilities quite variable between financial institutions, but in addition, there are different legal limitations placed on the investment opportunities of the intermediaries. If an intermediary is legally permitted to hold only two types of assets, they can only be substitutes no matter how different their risk components. It is still important that each type of security be classified according to the underlying risk characteristics just described so that a general hypothesis can be formulated regarding the substitute-complement issue. These general hypotheses will be modified when each financial intermediary is analyzed separately.

RELATIONSHIPS BETWEEN SECURITIES

When an analysis of the relationship between different securities is being undertaken, it is possible to classify them according to either (1) maturity or (2) issuer and/or the nature and priorities of claims. Short-term and long-term Government securities are differentiated by their term-to-maturity, while long-term Government bonds and long-term corporate bonds are distinguished by issuer. The major concern of this study is the question of the substitutability between securities classified according to the second characteristic just enumerated, disregarding the maturity distinction. In other words, our problem is to test the substitutability betweeen Government bonds, state-local bonds (municipals), corporate bonds, and mortgages that are homogeneous with respect to maturity; that is, each group contains securities either from all maturity ranges or from one particular maturity range. This by-passes certain interesting issues connected with the theory of the term structure of interest rates. Although it is correct to point out that our approach is capable of resolving the questions raised in Chapter 1, regarding the efficacy of monetary policy and the allocative function of the capital markets, the additional question of substitutability between different maturities of any one category of security would have been an interesting one to examine. Unfortunately, all attempts at approaching the term structure problem in our context were fruitless.

Before proceeding to discuss the risk relationship between the different groups of assets without regard to the effect of term-to-maturity, it will be useful to make one further observation on the maturity distinction. It should be noted that the major effect of maturity on the risk associated with securities occurs through uncertainty with respect to future interest rates. The effect of changing rates on the capital values of long-term securities is greater than the effect on the capital values of short-term securities.[2] Short-term securities have greater certainty with regard to capital value than do long-term securities, making them less risky, in this respect, than "longs."

The following groups of securities shall be examined with reference to their susceptibility to the five categories of uncertainty mentioned in the beginning of the first section of this chapter: (1) U.S. Government bonds, (2) corporate bonds, (3) state-local government bonds, (4) mortgages, and (5) equities. The first type of uncertainty relates to the loss of purchasing power when the price level rises, suffered by assets whose face value is fixed in money terms. The threat of inflation is a risk that all bondholders share together, as opposed to holders of real assets or the equity shares issued by corporations. The purchasing power risk differentiates the four categories of debt just listed from equity capital. It is possible to protect oneself from inflation to some extent by holding both equities and bonds (or just equities) in the portfolio.

[2] See [38] for a rigorous discussion of the effects of maturity on the behavior of interest rates and bond prices. An additional point is made in [47].

The uncertainty of the capital value of bonds because of the possibility of interest rate fluctuations is a second type of risk that differentiates equity and debt instruments. The fact that capital losses will be incurred on bonds, if liquidated, when future rates of interest increase will again encourage the holdings of equities (and/or cash) as a hedge against rising yields on bonds.

The risk of default is the major distinguishing feature between the liabilities of the Federal Government and the debts of all other institutions. Corporate bonds, municipals, mortgages (those not insured by the FHA) and equities all contain the risk of possible default. It is quite difficult to rank the different securities according to relative default risk. All the high-grade issues of these debtors are, perhaps, good substitutes for Governments on default risk grounds. The poorer-quality issues cannot be judged as easily for their relative default risk.

The uncertainty connected with the marketability of an asset is strongly influenced by the existence of a well-organized secondary market. Roland Robinson discusses briefly the secondary markets for Government bonds, corporate bonds, mortgages, municipals, and equities.[3] For example, it is clear that corporate equities have a very good secondary market. The organized stock exchanges, where a large number of equities are traded, are prime examples of well-organized secondary markets. Because we have established a fairly clear risk distinction between equities and bonds, the more interesting question is the relationship between the secondary markets of the various debt instruments.

There is little doubt that the secondary market for the securities of the U.S. Government is the best secondary market. The secondary markets for municipals and corporates are in a close tie with each other for "second place." The mortgage secondary market runs a very poor third. There has been no rigorous analysis of the relative efficiency of the secondary bond markets. This would be a worthwhile study. Until such a research project is undertaken, however, the crude ranking given by Robinson will have to suffice. Given this information regarding the secondary markets of debt instruments, we can say that the marketability risk is a clearly distinguishing feature when comparing Governments and mortgages.

COMPLEMENTS OR SUBSTITUTES?

The implications that are forthcoming from our discussion about the uncertainties associated with different categories of financial assets are

---

[3] The secondary markets are discussed in [44], pp. 19, 159, 222, and 256.

fairly straightforward. The uncertainties undertaken with the ownership of equity capital are quite independent of the uncertainties associated with bond ownership. This makes equities and all classes of debt instruments candidates for a possible complementary relationship.[4]

A clear distinction also emerges between mortgages and at least one other category of debt. The relative illiquidity of mortgages (rooted in the lack of a secondary market of any consequence) in comparison with Governments is quite marked. This implies that mortgages and Governments might be complements, even though they share similar risks because of inflation and the course of future interest rates. An increase in the holdings of mortgages (because of an increase in yield) by a financial intermediary might encourage an increase in the holdings of Governments in order to maintain a desired liquidity position, at the expense of a third group of securities. What is this third group of securities? Perhaps it is corporate bonds and/or municipals. Corporates and municipals do not share the excellent secondary-market characteristic of Governments. These secondary markets are poor in comparison with that of Government bonds. The major liquidity distinction, therefore, between mortgages and Governments simply does not exist when comparing mortgages with corporate bonds and municipals. The relationships between mortgages and these other two debt categories are probably ones of substitutability rather than complementarity.

Similar reasoning ought to imply that Government bonds are substitutes for both municipals and corporates. All three debt instruments share the purchasing power risk and interest rate risk. In contrast with mortgages, the secondary-market distinction, although important, does not seem to be the overbearing factor in the relationship between these two securities and Governments. Although it is also true that default risk separates Government bonds from corporate debt and municipals, the quality of bonds that financial institutions consider for investment makes the default risk a secondary consideration.

The relationship between corporate bonds and municipals is probably one of substitutability rather than complementarity. They both share very similar risks and, hence, might serve the same purpose in an investor's portfolio. There is one qualification, however, that must be pointed out. We have not mentioned the fact that the interest on state-local bonds is tax free. This feature of municipals does not really belong in the category of risk or uncertainty connected with bond holding except to

---

[4] The precise definition of substitute and complement as applied to relationships between securities is found in the section, "Introduction to Testing the Hypothesis," of this chapter.

the extent that tax rates might be altered in the future, thus creating uncertainty over the relative tax advantage of holding municipals. Because this risk does not persist in the normal course of events, a discussion of the tax status of municipals and its implications was deferred until now.

The fact that state-local bonds are tax-free makes them a unique and profitable investment for the institutions (and individuals) whose income is subject to full taxation under the corporate (individual) income tax. In fact, there are only two major financial intermediaries that actually hold significant amounts of municipals. Commercial banks and property and casualty insurance companies are the only intermediaries whose tax status greatly encourages the holdings of municipals.[5] For these institutions it might be expected that there be neither a substitute nor a complement relationship between municipals and corporates. (In reality non-life insurance companies and commercial banks simply do not hold very many corporate bonds.) Were it not for the tax-exemption, it is very likely that municipals and corporate bonds would be good substitutes in any portfolio.

It should be noted at this point that although the theoretical evaluation of substitutability and complementarity just completed included equities in the discussion, the empirical work in Chapter 3 shall not be addressed to the equity-bond relationship. As shall be pointed out later, the data on equity holdings is too poor to use even as a first approximation. The theoretical discussion included equities just in order to be complete and to set the groundwork for future research into this question when the appropriate data can be gathered.

INTRODUCTION TO TESTING THE HYPOTHESIS

The hypothesis that we have chosen to test is that different categories of securities are good substitutes for one another in the portfolios of financial intermediaries. As was pointed out in the previous section of this chapter, the a priori relationship between certain securities is hypothesized as complementarity rather than as substitutability. In either case, it is imperative that we formulate a rigorous definition of substitutes and complements as applied to different categories of securities, one that will also lend itself to empirical testing.

Two commodities, i and j are substitutes if $\delta Q_i / \delta P_j$ is positive, that is, *ceteris paribus*, an increase in the price (P) of good j induces an increase

[5] See [25], pp. 187–207.

in the demand (Q) for good i.[6] Traditional demand theory actually distinguishes between gross and net substitutes, the former including the income effect of the price change in the definition of substitutes and the latter being net of the income effect.[7] We shall return to the net-versus-gross distinction when we discuss the empirical counterpart to the substitution definition. The substitution term must be translated from the commodity market to the securities market. The obvious approach is to define two securities as substitutes if $\delta Q_a/\delta P_b$ is positive, where Q_a is the demand for security A and P_b is the price of the security B. For convenience the substitute relationship between securities is best discussed in terms of interest rates. Because security prices are inversely related to interest rates, two securities would be substitutes if $\delta Q_a/\delta i_b$ is negative, where i_b is the rate of interest on security B. Similarly, two securities are complements if $\delta Q_a/\delta i_b$ is positive.

There is at least one qualification that must be taken into account in the extension of the definition of substitutes from the goods market to the market for securities. Consumer demand theory typically abstracts from the effect of expectations on the demands for different goods. The role of expected interest rates cannot be ignored, however, while discussing the demands for securities. Clearly, changes in current rates of interest may influence expected future rates, which in turn may affect the demands for securities in the current period. This effect should also be included in the substitution term. In other words, $\delta Q_a/\delta i_b$ should include the effect of i_b on Q_a (or on Q_b, when discussing $\delta Q_b/\delta i_b$) through its effect on expected rates of interest. Because interest rates on securities (of similar maturity) are expected to move together, it is quite likely that the effect of expected changes in interest rates may cancel each other in the relative demands for two securities.

Given the above definition of substitutes and complements as applied to securities, it now remains to formulate an empirical counterpart to these terms. It is known that the regression coefficients of an estimated equation are interpreted as partial derivatives.[8] The coefficient a_1 of an explanatory variable X_1 implies that a unit change in X_1 will induce a change of a_1 times that unit in the dependent variable, holding all other explanatory variables in the equation constant. If one specifies a demand equation for a particular security and includes as arguments the own rate of interest, rates on other securities, and some portfolio constraint (the con-

---

[6] See [28], p. 29.

[7] The distinction between gross and net substitutes is presented most clearly in [35], pp. 76 and 103.

[8] See [30], pp. 52–61, and [34], pp. 18–19.

sumer is constrained by income, while a financial institution might be constrained by total liabilities), the estimated coefficients of the non-own rates are to be interpreted as (say) $\delta Q_a / \delta i_b$. This, indeed, is the precise term that tells us whether A and B are substitutes or complements in the particular investment portfolio. It is not that obvious whether this term corresponds to the gross or net concept of substitutes.

Let us see whether the income effect (when dealing with changes in a rate of interest this refers to the effect of such a change on the purchasing power of a dollar plus, perhaps, its effect on the capital value of the investment portfolio and how these affect the demand for the security) is relevant for a financial institution's demand for a security. In the theory of the firm, it is usually emphasized that, in contrast with the theory of the consumer, there is no income effect because there is no budget constraint. However, the situation to be considered here seems to be quite different for at least two reasons. As will be seen in the next section of this chapter, it is assumed that the intermediaries take the flow of deposits (liabilities) as given, that is, as a constraint similar to the consumer's budget constraint. Furthermore, a firm's demand for financial assets is probably quite different from its demand for inputs in the productive process. Although the firm's scale of production is not limited by any kind of budget constraint, its holdings of financial assets are probably limited by some type of wealth constraint (as long as a firm cannot issue its own debt indefinitely to finance its demands for financial assets). Although the case regarding the firm that does not take its inflow of funds (deposits) as a constraint is not that clear, the financial intermediaries in our model are most likely subject to an income effect.

Given the existence of the income effect, can we say whether the estimated regression coefficients attached to the rates of interest include this income effect or not; that is, are we estimating gross or net substitutability? It seems correct to say that we are determining gross substitutability. Although we hold some measure of income or wealth constant in each equation, by including the stock of deposits (liabilities) as an explanatory variable, the effect of the rate of interest on the demand for a security, through its impact on the value of the firm's flow of income or its wealth, is clearly not excluded from the coefficient of the rate of interest.

It should be noted that when Wold and Jureen discuss estimation of commodity demand equations they point out that for market-demand equations there is no direct interpretation of the Slutsky equation, hence, no direct counterpart to the income effect on an individual consumer.[9] When Feige estimates demand equations for various financial assets, he

[9] See [52], pp. 23, 98–111, 116, and 242, and [17], p. 35.

assumes, in order to impose the condition that the substitution term is symmetrical between the demand equations for assets A and B, that the income effect is negligible, so that the coefficients of non-own rates of interest represent the net substitute concept.[10] Whether our notion is correct or Feige's interpretation is correct, it is clear that emperically we are interested in the impacts of changes in other rates of interest on the demand for a particular security, holding other relevant influences constant. We will return to the implications of estimating gross substitutability in Chapter 3.

SPECIFICATION OF THE DEMAND EQUATIONS

Previous empirical studies of behavior in the financial markets have used the stock adjustment principle as the basic format for the specification of demand equations for particular financial assets.[11] Our equations will also be based on this principle. The basic assumption is that the quarterly flows of each asset depend upon the difference between current and desired levels. In addition, it is posited that the quarterly flow only partially adjusts for this discrepancy. The desired holdings of a security in the portfolio of a financial intermediary should be a function of the relative rates of interest on the various potential assets, a wealth constraint, such as the total assets (deposits) of the particular institution, and certain nonprice factors such as goodwill or public interest. Furthermore, certain types of institutional peculiarities and legal constraints might also enter as arguments in specific demand functions. The stock adjustment formulation can be represented as follows:

$$\Delta X_t = a \ (X_t^* - X_{t-1}) \tag{I}$$

where $0 < a < 1$, ΔX_t refers to the flow (for a particular portfolio) into security X during time period t $(X_t - X_{t-1})$, X_t^* represents the desired holdings of security X, and X_{t-1} is the amount of security X held in the portfolio of the particular intermediary at the end of last period. The desired level of security X in the intermediary's portfolio can be expressed most generally (according to the previous discussion) as follows:

$$X_t^* = b_1 + b_j \ [i_j] + b_{j+n}A \tag{II}$$

where $[i_j]$ is a set of interest rates that is relevant for the intermediary's

---

[10] Feige wants these results because the theorem proving that substitution effects are symmetrical applies only to net substitutes. See [17], pp. 7 and 35.

[11] For a discussion of the application of the stock adjustment principle to the demand for financial assets, see [22] Chapter II, pp. 31–38, and [12].

choice regarding portfolio composition, and A is the level of assets. Substituting (II) into (I) and adding X_{t-1} to each side produces

$$X_t = \alpha_1 + \alpha_2 A + \alpha_j [i_j] + \alpha_{j+n} X_{t-1} \qquad \text{(III)}$$

Equation III can be considered the general form of the demand for security X by a particular intermediary. As was just emphasized, it is quite probable that additional variables would be added to describe particular characteristics of each institution.

It is important to note at this point that most theoretical discussions of portfolio analysis demonstrate that the correct specification of security demand equations (with interest rates as explanatory variables) requires that the dependent variable be the ratio of X to total assets.[12] This means that Equation III should have X_t/A as the dependent variable. Many empirical studies of portfolio behavior have, however, used the linear formulation expressed in (III).[13] The investigators that have compared the linear and ratio forms have found little difference between the two.[14] Perhaps for equations that describe "short-run" behavior the linear specification is a reasonable approximation to the "theoretically more correct" ratio form. In the empirical work set forth below, both linear and ratio forms will be tried for each behavioral relationship, and the "better" equations, based on certain a priori criteria, will be used as final equations.

It was suggested before that both current interest rates and expected future rates ought to be reflected in evaluating substitute-complement relationships. We have not included expected rates as arguments in our equations for a number of reasons. The usual proxy for expected rates has been a weighted average of past interest rates.[15] The lagged dependent variable in the regression equations, however, actually incorporates a particular weighted average of past rates (and all other explanatory variables). Furthermore, what are really needed are expectations with regard to differential movements in the various interest rates that are relevant for a portfolio decision. Given that all rates tend to move together, it is quite probable that expectations effects tend to cancel out in our type of security demand equations (recall that we are not dealing with differences in maturity where expectations probably play a very strong role).

A number of other questions arise in light of the general specification of the demand equations that require clarification. First, should not the portfolio flows of other securities be used as explanatory variables in the

---

[12] See [43].
[13] See [22] and [15].
[14] See [22], Chapter V.
[15] See [12].

demand equations for any particular security? Certainly if an institution decides to increase its holdings of mortgages this may very well influence its demand for corporate bonds. Second, how is the balance sheet identity accounted for by the demand equations of each financial institution?

As far as the first question is concerned, it is undeniable that decisions with regard to the flows of other securities influence the demand for any particular security. The set of factors just listed as affecting the present desired level of any asset, however, incorporates the underlying variables upon which this decision-making process rests. If these variables actually succeed in incorporating all the underlying factors, it is really redundant to include also in the equation the actual final decision regarding the flows of other securities. If, however, the flow of a particular asset in the portfolio of any intermediary is based on other considerations, besides those which have been represented directly in each equation (by the interest rates and so on), it might be correct to include these flows as explanatory variables in the demand equations.

The second question, regarding the balance sheet identity connecting the assets in any institution's portfolio, can be resolved as follows. If there are n assets in a portfolio and if the portfolio size is given, then only the demands for $n - 1$ of those assets are functionally independent. The demand for one asset or group of assets is determined as a residual by the balance sheet identity. The demands for the major items in each intermediary's portfolio will be determined by explicit demand equations that shall be estimated. The securities that are only small proportions of total assets are to be considered as residuals and can be determined by the balance sheet identity. Appendix C discusses the implications of explicitly imposing the balance sheet constraint on the portfolios in our model.[16]

There are a number of theoretical points that we have not yet covered in this chapter. Because they are connected with the actual estimation of the equations and the data to be used, it will be more appropriate to discuss these issues in the beginning of Chapter 3.

---

[16] This also relates to the Brainard-Tobin conditions set forth in [7] regarding the internal consistency of a model of portfolio behavior. Our portfolio demand equations are also subjected to these tests in Chapter 3.

Chapter 3

ESTIMATION OF DEMAND EQUATIONS FOR SECURITIES

THE DATA

In this chapter, demand equations for the different securities held by various financial intermediaries will be specified. Each institution will be given separate treatment to allow for the expected variation in behavior patterns. Before proceeding to the analysis of each intermediary, a brief description of the data that shall be used in the actual estimation of the equations should be presented.

The Federal Reserve Flow of Funds Accounts (F/F) provides a comprehensive set of tables describing the flow of funds through the entire economy. This is the source of the data for all the asset and liability categories of each financial institution. The F/F data give the net flows and levels of liabilities and assets on a quarterly basis for each financial intermediary for the period between the first quarter of 1952 until the present. The data used in this study are seasonally unadjusted quarterly flows (and stocks) for the period covering the first quarter of 1953 through the fourth quarter of 1965. A description of the other data and their sources may be found in Appendix D.

There is one problem with the flow of funds data that must be pointed out. The security categories for which the quarterly flows are given are not differentiated according to maturity except for Government bonds. In other words, the change in holdings of municipals, corporates, and so on are not broken down into maturity groups. The objective in this study is to test the substitutability between different groups of securities that are homogeneous with regard to maturity. If two categories of assets differ with regard to maturity, in addition to the differentiation according to issuer and/or collateral, the hypothesis that we are attempting to test will not be resolved. If it is possible to argue that even these general categories of securities within each financial intermediary in the F/F tables are homogeneous with regard to maturity, then we are correct in using this set of data to test our stated hypothesis. It is our contention, to be justified later, that the assumption that different categories of securities of a financial intermediary are homogeneous with regard to maturity is a reasonable approximation to reality. If this is the case, then it is possible to use in our equations rates of interest referring to identical maturity ranges to represent the prospective yields obtainable on each category of assets.

The assumption that the group of securities considered for the portfolio of a particular intermediary are homogeneous with regard to maturity requires that either of the following propositions be true: (1) financial institutions that consider one particular maturity range when investing in (say) Government bonds, also consider only that maturity range for (say) corporates or (2) financial institutions that specialize in no particular maturity range of (say) Government bonds also are indifferent with respect to the maturity range of (say) corporates.

The one possible argument against these propositions is as follows. If institutions, such as life insurance companies or mutual savings banks, usually like to invest in long-term securities but hold Government bonds for liquidity, they may hold primarily short-term rather than long-term Governments, because "shorts" are more liquid than "longs." A casual glance at the maturity structure of Government bonds for each intermediary reveals the unimportance of this argument. For mutual savings banks, the holdings of short-term Government bonds (less than one year to maturity) averaged less than 7 percent of the total holdings of Governments between 1950 and 1965. The percentage ranged from a low of .8 percent in 1950 to 11 percent in 1965.[1] These figures indicate that although it may be worthwhile to analyze the issue of the substitutability between different maturities of Government bonds in the portfolios of mutual savings banks, the use of the long-term bond rate as the representative yield on the mutual savings banks' portfolio of Governments in conjunction with (say) the corporate bond rate is a justified procedure.

The implications of the percentage maturity distribution of the Gov-

---

[1] See [40], p. 187 and Federal Reserve Bulletins (June 1965, p. 859).

ernment bond holdings of life insurance companies are quite similar to those drawn from mutual savings banks. Life insurance company holdings of short-term Government bonds (less than one year to maturity) varied between 6 and 8 percent of total holdings of Governments between 1952 and 1964.[2] The same maturity breakdown, that is, very small holdings of short-term Governments, is found for all financial intermediaries except commercial banks. Even among commercial banks, over 60 percent of Government bond holdings are in the above-one-year category. An attempt will be made, however, to explain the maturity composition of the Government bond portfolio of commercial banks. With all other institutions, however, it seems quite appropriate to use the long-term rates as the relevant interest rates for portfolio choice.

INTEREST RATES IN THE EQUATIONS

Let us now turn to the form in which the interest rate variables will appear in the demand equations and to the precise test we shall use to ascertain whether the various securities are substitutes or complements or are independent. The effect of interest rates on the demands for securities by financial institutions is most clearly revealed by the following quotation with regard to the behavior of life insurance companies: "shifts in the *differential* on net yields on bonds versus mortgages typically are reflected in the direction of new investments."[3] The relevant information required by the portfolio manager in the decision-making process regarding the flow of investment funds in a single period seems to be interest-rate differentials rather than the absolute level of rates. A portfolio manager will be most concerned with the level of interest rates when the cash-versus-securities decision is being made.[4] Unlike most individuals whose transactions demand for cash is sensitive to the level of interest rates, financial intermediaries typically hold the minimum level of cash that is compatible with the level of their liabilities, regardless of whether the interest rate is 3 percent or 5 percent. An example of the behavior of the cash holdings of an intermediary is seen in the portfolios of savings and loan associations where cash holdings went from $.3 billion to $2.7 billion during the 1950–1960 period, varying directly with the size of total deposits. It also may be noted that cash is an extremely small portion of

[2] This point is also made in [45], pp. 90–91.
[3] See [37], p. 65. Also see [40], p. 127, for a similar emphasis on the influence of rate differentials on mutual savings bank investment.
[4] See [5] for a discussion of interest elasticity of transactions for cash.

financial intermediary portfolios, as is evidenced by the following percentages of cash in some typical portfolios at the end of 1960: mutual savings banks, 2.2; savings and loan associations, 3.8; life insurance companies, 1.1.[5]

These factors seem to permit the use of interest rate differentials rather than the levels of rates as arguments in the security demand equations. The ability to use rate differentials might prove to be very important from a statistical standpoint because the levels of all the interest rates are quite collinear. The existence of multicollinearity could prevent the emergence of statistically significant regression coefficients. Therefore, our security demand equations will be specified using both interest rate levels and, as an alternative, interest rate differentials.

It should be noted that entering the interest rates into the equations in differential form imposes a restriction on the sign of the own rate. In particular, if we estimate $a_1 (i_{CB} - i_{GB})$ and $a_2 (i_M - i_{GB})$ in a demand equation for Government bonds (where i_{CB} is the corporate bond rate, i_M is the mortgage rate, and i_{GB} is the Government bond rate), the sign of i_{GB} equals $-(a_1)$ plus $-(a_2)$, or the negative of the sum of the coefficients attached to i_{CB} and i_M, respectively. The use of differentials also implies that if some factor k were added to each rate, the distribution of funds among alternative securities in the investment portfolios of financial intermediaries would remain unchanged. Although this behavioral result follows from the use of differentials (and that can be justified by our assumption regarding the holding of cash balances by intermediaries), it should be noted that it is also quite possible to present other reasonable behavioral assumptions that imply the use of the levels of the interest rates rather than differentials. Indeed, if we were to use the levels, we would be sacrificing only a degree of freedom in the estimation procedure and be gaining the elimination of the restrictions just described. For this reason, we shall prefer, in general, the specification using levels rather than differentials if the multicollinearity problem does not prove to be severe.

Let us now discuss the criteria we shall use (1) to evaluate the reasonableness of our equations and (2) to test whether the securities in the portfolios of our intermediaries are substitutes or complements or are independent. In evaluating the performance of our equations, in addition to examining the correlation coefficient and the standard error of estimate, we shall place strong emphasis on whether the estimated coefficients have signs that agree with a priori specification. We shall be able to test also whether the restriction on the coefficient of the own rate when using rate differentials results in incorrect estimates by examining the implicit sign

[5] See [40], p. 102.

of the own rate of interest. This consistency check requires that the own rate coefficient derived from our estimated coefficients of the rate differentials be positive in sign. Tests will also be conducted to examine the consistency of one estimated equation with the others in the model. A detailed description of these consistency checks is reserved for discussion in the section on mutual savings banks.

The criterion that will be used to test whether two securities are substitutes or complements or are independent is as follows. Assume that we estimate the demand for Government bonds, as just specified, and produce the following two interest rate terms: $a_1 (i_{CB} - i_{GB})$ and $a_2 (i_M - i_{GB})$. If the coefficient of (say) i_{CB} (that is, a_1), is negative in sign and significant at the 5 percent level, we conclude that this equation implies that the two securities (corporates and Governments) are substitutes. If the sign of a_1 were positive and the coefficient were significant, then the two securities would be considered complements. If the ratio of the coefficient to its standard error (the t-value) were very small, for example, less than .5, then this equation would imply that the two securities were independent in demand.

If the t-value of a correctly signed coefficient were less than 1, we might still consider this as supporting a substitute or complement relationship if there were significant evidence from the equation describing the symmetrical relationship. For example, in the demand equation for corporate bonds a coefficient for $(i_{GB} - i_{CB})$ is estimated. If its coefficient is negative and significant, we conclude also that there is a substitute relationship between corporates and Governments. In such a case we can use the correctly signed but very insignificant coefficient from the Government bond demand equation as supporting evidence. It is expected that the relationship described between two securities gleaned from one equation will agree with the implications from the equation describing the symmetrical relationship. Although this is not a strict requirement from the theoretical point of view (because only when using the concept of *net* substitutes is it required that the substitution effects be symmetrical), it is still a desirable property to request of the results.

Let us now set forth the conclusions to be drawn when a significant relationship is produced in one equation, (say) implying substitutability, and conflicting evidence results from the equation dealing with the symmetrical relationship. It seems reasonable to say that if we have a significant relationship, for example, substitutability, from one equation and an insignificant complementary relationship from the other, we conclude that the significant coefficient describes the appropriate relationship. If the two equations imply conflicting results with similar t-values for both relevant coefficients, then we are forced to disregard both implications.

In Chapter 2 and the first two sections of this chapter an attempt was made to lay the theoretical foundations for the portfolio choice between different categories of securities by financial intermediaries. The precise specification of each demand equation was not attempted, and it is to this topic we now turn.

The equations presented here are estimated using the two-stage least squares (TSLS) procedure. The predetermined variables used in the first stage regressions come from the exogenous variables of the entire model. The complete set of structural equations will appear in Chapter 4. Because the entire model contains over eighty predetermined variables, a subset of instrumental variables was picked and used to generate the values of the codetermined variables in the first stage of the TSLS procedure. The criteria set forth by Fisher[6] for choosing instrumental variables in economy-wide econometric models were used as general guidelines in eliminating potential predetermined variables from the "first-stage." For example, only one lagged endogenous variable was used in the first-stage regressions. The predetermined variables used in almost all of the regressions are (1) unborrowed reserves plus currency (Z), (2) the discount rate (i_D), (3) the maximum time deposit rate (i_{MTD}), (4) capacity utilization (CU), (5) manufacturers' unfilled orders (MUO), (6) GNP lagged one period (Y_{-1}), (7) government expenditure (G), (8) the rate of change in prices $(\Delta P/P)$, (9) the supply of state-local bonds $(\overline{SL})$, (10) assets of life insurance companies (A^1), (11) assets of pension plans (A^p), and (12) household formation (ΔHH). Unless otherwise indicated, all of the equations set forth below were estimated using TSLS with the data covering the period 1953, first quarter, through 1965, fourth quarter. All the dollar magnitudes are expressed in *millions* of dollars, and the interest rates are in percent (for example, 2.00). The flow variables (for example, GNP, investment) are expressed as quarter-to-quarter changes and are not at annual rates.

MUTUAL SAVINGS BANKS

AN INTRODUCTION

Mutual savings banks (MSB) are thrift institutions located primarily in the northeast section of the United States. The legal restrictions on their lending activities are somewhat mild in comparison with (say) savings and loan associations. They are permitted to hold most types of securities

---

[6] See [18].

except that equity holdings are restricted to a certain percentage of assets.[7] In point of fact, the overwhelming majority of MSB security holdings are divided among mortgages, Government bonds, and corporate bonds.[8] Governments are held primarily for liquidity while the other two debt instruments are held for their income.[9] The model specifies demand equations for these three categories of securities.

Before preceeding to discuss the specification of the equations, let us list the notation to be used in the discussion of mutual savings banks. The explanation of notation will take place at the beginning of each section so that the reader will have it close at hand upon examining the demand equations for each institution. Superscripts are attached to some variables to indicate to which intermediary the particular stock or flow corresponds. Each intermediary is represented by a letter as follows: U, mutual savings banks; S, savings and loan associations; C, commercial banks; P, pension plans; L, life insurance companies; O, other insurance companies. These letters only represent the particular institution when they appear as superscripts. The variables employed in the demand equations for mutual savings banks appear with the following notation:

GB^u: Government bonds (of mutual savings banks)

CB^u: Corporate bonds (of mutual savings banks)

M^u: Mortgages (of mutual savings banks)

D^u: Deposits (of mutual savings banks)

i_{GB}:   Interest rate on long-term (above ten years to maturity) Government bonds

i_{CB}:   Interest rate on corporate bonds

i_M: Interest rate on mortgages

---

[7] The legal framework within which mutual savings banks must operate is discussed in [40], pp. 103–108. Although only 6 out of 17 states actually prohibit equity holdings by mutual savings banks, there are strict limitations that curb effective portfolio use of this capital market instrument (see p. 108).

[8] The percentage distribution of assets in the portfolios of savings banks is found in [40], p. 102. At the end of 1960, they held 15.4 percent (of assets) in Governments, 1.7 percent in municipals, 12.5 percent in corporate bonds, 65.8 percent in mortgages, and the remainder in cash and other assets. The percentage distribution remained fairly constant through the end of the sample period (except that Governments continued to decline as a percentage of total assets).

[9] See [40], pp. 109–110.

S_i: Seasonal dummy variables for which $i = 1,2,3$; each variable
takes on a value of 1 for the quarter represented by its subscript and is zero elsewhere

A complete description of the data and the sources is found in
Appendix D. The flow of any variable will be indicated by a capital
delta (Δ). If there are any lags the variables will be subscripted and the
appropriate quarterly lag will be indicated.

MUTUAL SAVINGS BANK DEMAND EQUATIONS

Because we shall be analyzing six financial institutions, it is impossible
to fully discuss the nature and particular characteristics of each one. We
hope to present the factors that directly influence the choice of which
variables to enter into each equation.

The general form of a demand equation makes the holdings of a
particular security a function of the lagged holdings of that security, the
interest rates, and a set of constraint variables. In addition, seasonal
dummy variables are included in order to account for independent seasonal patterns in the demand for any security. The first question that
must be resolved is the particular constraints that should be imposed
on the demand equations. The total assets or liabilities of an institution
certainly qualify as constraints in the demand equations for each category of security. The flow of total assets might also enter the demand
equations where initial and long-run reactions have a sharp discontinuity.
In the demand equations for mutual savings banks, total deposits will
be viewed as a portfolio constraint variable.

Because the major items in MSB portfolios are Government bonds,
corporate bonds, and mortgages, the interest rates that are candidates
for inclusion in the demand equations are the respective rates on these
securities. Given this brief introduction to the behavior pattern of savings
banks, it seems most appropriate to set forth the final estimated equations, after which an extensive discussion of the results will be presented.
Below the coefficient of each variable the t-value (ratio of the coefficient
to its standard error) is enclosed in parentheses. A number of statistical
measures describing various characteristics of the relationship in the
estimated equation are also given below the entire equation. They are
R^2, the percentage of variance that is explained; SE, the standard error
of estimate; SE/DV, the standard error divided by the mean of the
dependent variable; DW, the Durbin-Watson statistic; and RHO, the
estimated coefficient in the autoregressive equation used to difference

the original variables when necessary.[10] The estimated equations are as follows:

$$GB^u = 280.8\ i_{GB} - 116.0\ i_{CB} + .458\ \Delta D^u - .029\ D^u$$
$$\quad\quad (3.13) \quad\quad (1.73) \quad\quad\quad (5.46) \quad\quad\quad (4.60)$$
$$+\ .916\ GB^u_{-1} + 195.0\ S_1 + 35.5\ S_2$$
$$\quad (22.0) \quad\quad\quad (4.62) \quad\quad (1.28)$$
$$+\ 90.9\ S_3 + 82.9$$
$$\quad (2.73) \quad\quad (1.35)$$
$$R^2 = .99 \quad\quad\quad SE/DV = .010$$
$$SE = 69.3 \quad\quad\quad DW = 1.92$$

(1)

$$CB^u = 456.2\ i_{CB} - 559.4\ i_{GB} + .009\ D^u + .808\ CB^u_{-1}$$
$$\quad\quad (3.54) \quad\quad (3.00) \quad\quad\quad (1.46) \quad\quad (9.76)$$
$$-\ 50.8\ S_1 - 7.1\ S_2 - 14.1\ S_3 + 221.1$$
$$\quad (.77) \quad\quad (.11) \quad\quad (.22) \quad\quad\quad (1.10)$$
$$R^2 = .83 \quad\quad\quad SE/DV = .052$$
$$SE = 164.6 \quad\quad\quad DW = 1.89$$

(2)

$$M^u/D^u = -\ .013\ (i_{CB} - i_M) + .009\ (i_{GB} - i_M)$$
$$\quad\quad\quad (5.34) \quad\quad\quad\quad (4.78)$$
$$+\ .89\ (M^u/D^u)_{-1} - .11\ (GB^u/D^u)_{-1}$$
$$\quad (25.7) \quad\quad\quad\quad\quad (2.94)$$
$$-\ .008\ S_1 - .001\ S_2$$
$$\quad (9.78) \quad\quad (1.67)$$
$$-\ .003\ S_3 + .103$$
$$\quad (3.59) \quad\quad (3.37)$$
$$R^2 = .99 \quad\quad\quad SE/DV = .003$$
$$SE = .002 \quad\quad\quad DW = 1.65$$

(3)

Let us examine each equation separately (with regard to the sub-stitute-complement issue, the speed of adjustment, and the relevant constraint variables) and then discuss their general implications for mutual savings bank behavior. The demand for Governments (Equation 1) implies that Government bonds and corporate bonds are substitutes for each other in MSB portfolios. The coefficient of i_{CB} has a negative

[10] If the Durbin-Watson statistic indicates that the residuals of an equation are autocorrelated, we estimate the autoregressive equation (of the residuals) in order to get the coefficient, RHO, which is used to difference all the variables in the original equation. Using this transformed set of variables, we re-estimate the original equation in order to produce estimates that do not have to be qualified because of serial cor-

sign and is significant using a one-tailed test at the 5 percent level. When the mortgage rate (i_M) was entered into the equation, it had a positive coefficient with a t-value of .83. When ($i_M - i_{GB}$) and ($i_{CB} - i_{GB}$) were entered instead of the levels of rates, the former had a positive coefficient with a t-value of 1.41, and the latter had a negative coefficient with a t-value of 1.97. Although the results just described imply that mortgages and Governments are quite likely complementary in demand, as had been hypothesized above, we chose to surpress the i_M variable in the "final" version of Equation 1 because it was obvious that the a priori substitute relationship between corporates and Governments was dominant. We shall return to the evidence regarding complementarity when discussing Equation 3, the demand for mortgages.

The speed of adjustment implied by the coefficient of the lagged dependent variable in Equation 1 suggests that about 9 percent of the discrepancy between actual and desired holdings of Governments is eliminated during the first quarter, or approximately 30 percent of adjustment takes place within one year. This speed of adjustment is much faster than that found in the security demand equations estimated in previous models of the financial sector.[11]

The deposit variable enters Equation 1 both as a stock and as a flow. The negative sign attached to D^u implies that during the period covered in our model, Government bonds might be called an "inferior" asset; that is, the demand declined as MSB deposits increased. The most reasonable explanation is that the large amount of Governments held at the end of World War II were far in excess of desired levels and that these holdings were sold off gradually until the present to finance (say)

---

relation. For example, if we estimate

$$Y_t = a_1 X_t + a_2 Z_t + U_t$$

and DW indicates significant autocorrelation in the residual (U), we proceed to estimate

$$U_t = (RHO) U_{t-1} + E_t$$

We then re-estimate the behavioral equation in the following form:

$$Y_t - (RHO) Y_{t-1} = b_1 [X_t - (RHO) X_{t-1}] + b_2 [Z_t - (RHO) Z_{t-1}] + e_t$$

This procedure removes the undesirable autocorrelation from the estimated equation. In the rest of this study, whenever an equation is transformed in this manner, we shall report the value of RHO used in the transformation below the estimated results. A full explanation of the method is found in [30], pp. 177–199.

[11] See [22] and [12].

increased mortgage holdings. The positive sign attached to ΔD^u implies that during the first period of a deposit inflow the funds are put initially into Government bonds and then in the following period are taken out of Governments and put into the remaining assets of the portfolio. When ΔD^u was not included in the equation, the DW-statistic indicated positive serial correlation.

The demand for corporate bonds (Equation 2) confirms the fact that Governments and corporates are good substitutes for each other in mutual savings bank portfolios. When the mortgage rate was entered into the equation either in level form or as a rate differential, its coefficient had a very insignificant t-value (less than .5). The speed of adjustment in corporate bond demand is about 20 percent in the first quarter or about 60 percent after one year. The constraint variable is the level of deposits, D^u. It has a small positive coefficient that is significant only at the 10 percent level using a one-tailed test. The small size of this coefficient (and its borderline significance) is not surprising because MSB are investors in mortgages primarily. In 1965 corporate bonds made up only 5 percent of the total portfolio, while mortgages were over 75 percent of total assets.

The most striking difference between the demand equation for mortgages (Equation 3) and the two other MSB demand equations is the fact that the final version of M^u demand is a ratio to total assets while the two other equations for MSB are in linear form. Equation 3 is homogeneous in dollar magnitudes. As was mentioned in Chapter 2, the ratio-to-total-assets specification is theoretically more correct. All three equations for savings banks were tried in both linear and ratio form (as is the case with all of the demand equations to be reported). When GB^u and CB^u were put into ratio form, however, the speed of adjustment became infinite and the estimated coefficients made little sense. Only for mortgage demand did the ratio form seem most appropriate. These results suggest that the linear form might be a better approximation to short-run behavior in representing the demand for Governments and corporates while the ratio form is more appropriate in the mortgage demand equation.

The coefficients of the rate differentials in Equation 3 suggest that mortgages are complementary in demand with Governments whereas they are substitutes for corporate bonds. Note that the implicit coefficient of i_M is positive $(+.004)$, as is required by the consistency check described above. The speed of adjustment is similar to that of Equation 1 (although slightly faster), that is, a little over 10 percent after the first quarter and over 30 percent after one year. The lagged holdings of Governments appears in Equation 3 with a negative sign. Although a priori one might expect a positive coefficient (that is, the greater the holdings of Governments last period, the greater the current demand for mortgages), the coefficient of the $(GB^u/D^u)_{-1}$ variable reflects the falling trend in the ratio of Governments to total deposits and the rising trend in M^u/D^u. The negative sign is, therefore, most appropriate because the fall in Government bond holdings has actually financed (in part) increases in mortgage holdings. This is not, however, inconsistent with the evidence that mortgages and Governments are complementary in demand. As was mentioned before, the abnormally high level of Government bonds held at the end of World War II led to a continued decumulation of these securities by MSB through 1965. The evidence of complementarity suggests that the rate of accumulation of mortgages was sensitive to the level of the Government bond rate relative to the mortgage rate. It is only in a very simplified model, that is, where actual stocks always equal desired stocks, in which one can suggest (if at all) that complementarity implies that the actual holdings of two assets will move together. In our case this certainly need not be true.

Other terms of credit for mortgages were also tried as explanatory variables. The length of amortization and the loan-to-value ratio were tried, in particular, but the initial results were not significant. These variables were tried in the mortgage demand equations of other institutions, but they generally did not show up significantly.

The existence of a substitute relationship between Governments and corporates was corroborated by both Equations 1 and 2. The relationship is symmetrical. The complementarity between Governments and mortgages and the substitutability between corporates and mortgages are suggested by Equation 3 only. These relationships do not appear to be symmetrical in the final equations that were used. It was pointed out that from a strictly theoretical argument, one cannot require that these relationships be symmetrical; that is, we are measuring gross (of the income effect) substitutability and not net substitutability. It would have been more elegant, however, to have arrived at symmetrical substitutability and complementarity. The evidence from the mortgage demand equation is, nevertheless, quite strong because when i_{GB} and i_{CB} were not included in Equation 3, the sign of the mortgage rate (which remained) was negative and insignificant. When i_{GB} and i_{CB} were entered together so that their signs were constrained to be the same, the combined variable had a t-value close to zero.

One final note with regard to substitutability and complementarity concerns the use of regression slopes as opposed to elasticities. The elasticities of all security demands with respect to each interest rate for all institutions are recorded in Appendix A. In terms of identifying *statistically* significant substitutability or complementarity, it is sufficient to ascertain the statistical significance of the interest rate coefficients in the regression equations. Whether these regression slopes correspond to elasticities that are large or small in magnitude is a separate issue and will be discussed in Appendix A.

The overall performance of the regression equations describing MSB portfolio behavior is good. Although the high correlation coefficients might be expected because of the use of highly collinear time series data, the small standard errors in relationship to the means of the dependent variables indicate a strong set of regression equations. The DW statistics all indicate that there is no serial correlation, although the presence of lagged dependent variables in the equations sheds doubt on the strength of the test for autocorrelation.

The three security demand equations for MSB indicate that savings banks are responsive to interest rates in allocating funds among alternative investments. In order for these portfolio demands to be consistent with one another, the long-run allocation of a unit increase in deposits among the alternative investment opportunities ought to total near unity.[12] Because we shall use the point estimates of the deposit coefficients to calculate these figures, the summation ought to lie in the vicinity of unity, since one cannot expect exact results. Linearizing Equation 3 (at the values for 1965, fourth quarter) and setting all lagged variables equal to current levels to get long-run equilibrium values, the coefficient of D^u is .99. The long-run coefficient of D^u in Equation 2 is .04. The long-run coefficient of D^u in Equation 1 is approximately $-.35$. The sum of these is .68. In reality, however, the long-run coefficient of D^u in Equation 1 is much too large because there is obviously an upper limit to the decumulation of Governments. Even with this estimate, however, the three equations do describe a reasonable behavior pattern when taken together. Had the sum of the long-run coefficients added to 5.0 or .03, it would have been evident that our point estimates of the constraint variables were quite out of line.

There is one slight inconsistency in the set of equations that is related to the D^u variable. In Equation 1 there is evidence (discussed before) that initially almost one half of an increment to deposits is put into Governments and after one period there is a corresponding decrease in the holdings of Governments. This type of discontinuity is not found explicitly in any of the other estimated equations. Although mortgage demand continues to

---

[12] W. C. Brainard and J. Tobin in [7] suggest that consistency checks such as those conducted here are necessary to insure that individual equations of a model do not imply contradictory behavioral patterns.

increase in the period after an increment to deposits, it falls short of the coincident decrease in holdings of Governments. The only other possibility is that the holdings of some other asset whose demand is not represented by an explicit equation, such as equities or cash, receives part of the funds that are generated by the liquidation of Governments. This can partially explain the inconsistency, although the discrepancies involved are probably too large to be absorbed in equities alone. In all likelihood, the simple ΔD^u added to Equation 1 only approximates the more gradual shift of funds out of Governments and into other assets, for example, mortgages. Other studies of savings banks have found that funds go into cash and/or Governments initially and then are placed gradually into other earning assets.[13] Our results tend to corroborate these findings.

There is one other consistency check that has been suggested by Brainard and Tobin.[14] They argue that if wealth is held constant the interest rate effects on security demands ought to total zero for a given portfolio (they refer to the dynamic disequilibrium path as well as to initial impacts). Obviously, if one equation states that an increase in the corporate bond rate causes demand for corporates to rise by $200 million, then some other asset or group of assets in the portfolio must decrease by $200 million, assuming that wealth is constant. This requirement, however, can be applied only partially to the institutional demand equations of our model. First, as was mentioned before, there is an income effect of changes in rates, and, therefore, wealth (or the value of deposits) is not held constant. Second, the security demands that are explicit in (say) MSB portfolios make up only a portion of total assets (albeit a large portion). The "unwritten" equations for other portfolio items, in this case equities, cash, and other assets (which totalled to $5 billion at the end of 1965) together with the budget constraint can account for some of the obvious discrepancies in the estimated response of security demands to changes in interest rates. For mutual savings banks the first-period responses to changes in interest rates are as follows (when the mortgage demand equation is linearized at 1965, fourth quarter). When i_{GB} rises by 1 percentage point, GB^u increases by $281 million, CB^u falls by $559 million, and M^u rises by $524 million; the algebraic sum of these dollar responses is $244 million. When i_{CB} rises by 1 percentage point, GB^u falls by $116 million, CB^u rises by $456 million, and M^u falls by $757 million; the algebraic sum of these responses is (minus) $417 million. When i_M rises by 1 percentage point, M^u rises by $233 million, which also is the net effect of an increase in i_M.

[13] See [29].
[14] See [7].

There are a number of interesting conclusions forthcoming from these simple experiments. First, the largest discrepancy occurs with i_{CB}, which still turns out to be less than \$500 million. Second, the most obvious violation of the Brainard-Tobin test, namely, that i_M appears only in the M^u demand equation, produces the smallest dollar discrepancy. Third, the largest dollar problem, that is, that for changes in i_{CB}, turns out to produce a dollar discrepancy that is only 10 percent of the total value of "other assets" that are viewed as a residual. All these factors combine to indicate that although our point estimates of the interest rate coefficients may violate the strict requirements of the Brainard–Tobin conditions, they certainly can be considered relevant approximations within the model-building context. It is not unrealistic to assume that at least part of the discrepancies are accounted for by variations in the residual elements in the portfolios and part is accounted for by altering, within one standard error, the point estimates of the regression coefficients. These general conclusions also hold for the remaining set of financial intermediary portfolios except where indicated otherwise.

SAVINGS AND LOAN ASSOCIATIONS

AN INTRODUCTION

Savings and loan associations (SLA) are privately managed thrift and home-financing institutions that are usually organized as mutual associations, that is, owned by the savers. In contrast with mutual savings banks, SLA are located throughout the continental United States. Another distinguishing feature is the myriad of legal regulations imposed upon the investment portfolios of SLA. The overwhelming majority of associations are permitted to hold only mortgages, Government bonds, Federal National Mortgage Association (FNMA) debentures, and Federal Home Loan Bank consolidated notes. Certain state-chartered savings associations have the right to purchase municipal bonds (Federally chartered institutions do not have this power).[15] Between 1950 and 1960 the mortgage holdings of SLA varied from 80 percent of total assets to 85 percent of total assets, while Government bonds were between 6.2 and 8.8 percent of assets.[16] These figures indicate the importance of mortgages in the portfolios of savings and loan associations.

There is another important characteristic of savings associations that must be examined prior to the analysis of their investment behavior.

---

[15] See [32], p. 93.
[16] See [32], p. 82.

Both mutual savings banks and savings and loan associations have the right to borrow from the Federal Home Loan Bank (FHLB). Only SLA have used the borrowing facilities to any great extent. Mutual savings banks have a tradition against borrowing, whereas savings associations do not appear to have any significant aversion to requesting borrowed funds from the FHLB.[17] The interest rate charged by the FHLB should have an effect on the demand for funds similar to the effect of the discount rate charged to commercial banks by the Federal Reserve.

The major principle guiding the investment policies of SLA may be summed up with the following quotation: "As basically mutual thrift and home financing institutions, savings and loan associations have developed a strong public service raison d'être. They hold that their basic purpose is to serve the shelter needs of the American people."[18] The tradition of home mortgage lending is very strong in the investment objectives of savings associations. In addition, liquidity considerations and safety of the depositors' money are foremost in the minds of the officers of the savings associations. United States Government securities are considered the basic source of liquidity in the investment account of these institutions. They consider their bond investments as liquidity and consider speculation in the Government bond market as not advisable.[19]

There is one other legal prescription for the investment account of SLA. Holdings of cash plus United States Government securities must equal at least 7 percent of total savings and investment accounts. The interpretation of the coefficient of SLA deposits in the Government bond demand equation must, therefore, recognize the existence of this legal requirement. The deposit coefficient cannot be explained in simple behavioral terms.

SAVINGS AND LOAN ASSOCIATION DEMAND EQUATIONS

The demands for Governments and mortgages by savings and loan associations are the variables we shall attempt to explain in this section. The new notation that shall be employed in the estimated equations is as follows:

GB^s: Government bonds (of savings and loan associations)

M^s: Mortgages (of savings and loan associations)

[17] See [40], p. 41, and [32], pp. 120–121.
[18] See [32], p. 96.
[19] See [32], pp. 92–93.

D^s: Deposits (of savings and loan associations)

i_{FHLB}:   Interest rate charged by FHLB

The estimated demand equations for mortgages and Governments are

$$GB^s = 632.3\ i_{GB} - 79.2\ i_{FHLB} + .031\ D^s + .440\ GB^s_{-1}$$
$$(5.74) \qquad (2.12) \qquad (4.76) \qquad (3.90)$$
$$+\ 218.3\ S_1 + 42.5\ S_2 + 18.0\ S_3 - 1198.7$$
$$(5.98) \qquad (1.06) \qquad (.48) \qquad (4.98)$$
$$R^2 = .99 \qquad\qquad SE/DV = .02$$
$$SE = 92.3 \qquad\qquad DW = 1.67$$

(4)

$$M^s = -114.1\ i_{FHLB} + .380\ D^s + .639\ M^s_{-1} - 235.1\ S_1$$
$$(.91) \qquad\qquad (4.39) \qquad (7.30) \qquad\quad (4.40)$$
$$+\ 186.7\ S_2 + 486.7\ S_3 - 126.9$$
$$(2.19) \qquad (8.16) \qquad (.23)$$
$$R^2 = .99 \qquad\qquad SE/DV = .011$$
$$SE = 186.9 \qquad\qquad DW = 1.55$$
$$RHO = .73$$

(5)

The Government bond demand equation (Equation 4) suggests that changes in i_{GB} relative to i_{FHLB} affect SLA demand for Governments. Because the mortgage rate does not appear in Equation 4 (nor in Equation 5), it seems correct to conclude that mortgages and Governments are not substitutes in SLA portfolios. The hypothesized complementary relationship could not apply here because SLA can hold, essentially, only mortgages and Governments and in a "two-commodity world" only substitutability is possible. The significance of i_{GB} in Equation 4 suggests, therefore, that savings and loan associations increase their demand for Governments as i_{GB} rises and this most likely occurs at the expense of increased borrowings at the FHLB. The significant coefficient attached to D^s reflects, primarily, the legal requirement that Governments plus cash must equal at least 7 percent of total SLA assets. The speed of adjustment implies that 56 percent occurs after one quarter and over 90 percent of adjustment is completed during the first year.

Equation 5 describes SLA demand for mortgages. The own rate (i_M) does not appear as an explanatory variable. When it was entered into the equation, it had a negative coefficient. The FHLB borrowing rate does appear in the equation, although it is not significant. Prior to differencing the variables by RHO (calculated at .73), i_{FHLB} was significant in the version of Equation 5 that had autocorrelation. This factor plus the a priori expectation that i_{FHLB} would affect mortgage demand suggested that it should not be dropped from the M^s demand equation. The coefficient of the lagged dependent variable implies that 36 percent of adjustment occurs in the first period and about 80 percent of adjustment is completed after one year. The deposit variable is the relevant constraint on mortgage demand as it is with Government bond demand.

The overall performance of the two equations for SLA is rather good in terms of low standard errors. The fact that the autoregressive structure had to be estimated for Equation 5 indicates that although the statistical effects of serial correlation were eliminated, there is some relevant variable left out of the specification. This is most likely related to the "nonprice" factors influencing SLA demand for mortgages. In addition, this professed desire "to provide for the shelter needs of the public" can help to explain the lack of portfolio substitutability between mortgages and Governments revealed by Equations 4 and 5.

The long-run coefficients attached to the deposit variables in the two equations for SLA also reveal that the estimates are within reason. From Equation 4 the long-run coefficient of D^s is .05, and from Equation 5 the coefficient is 1.05. The sum of the two, 1.10, is quite close to unity. Although the point estimate of the coefficient of D^s in Equation 5 is obviously too large, the sum of the coefficients is well within a reasonable band around unity.

COMMERCIAL BANKS

AN INTRODUCTION

The literature on the portfolio behavior of commercial banks is voluminous.[20] There is little point in merely repeating the well-known regulations on bank portfolios, the relationship between Federal Reserve activity and bank profit maximization, and the importance of nonprice considerations in the management of bank funds. Our objective here is very specific, that is, to examine the degree to which different bank assets are substitutes for each other. In view of this goal, we shall follow the behavioral assumptions regarding bank portfolio activity made by Goldfeld in his econometric analysis of the banking system.[21]

There is one major portfolio regulation imposed on commercial banks that will be included in the specification of our equations but that was

---

[20] The portfolio behavior of commercial banks is the subject of [22], [46], and [1], especially pp. 121–297.
[21] See [22], Chapter II.

ignored by Goldfeld. All public deposits at commercial banks, that is, deposits of the Federal Government and of state-local governments, must be secured by "pledged" assets. There are two types of securities that can be used to secure public deposits; they are Government bonds (including agency bonds) and municipals (the categories that are eligible vary from state to state). In 1966 almost $50 billion of commercial bank assets were thus frozen, or about 45 percent of total investments.[22] This constraint must be made explicit in analyzing the portfolio behavior of commercial banks. Except for this change, the specification of the demand equations for banks will follow, somewhat closely, the assumptions made in the study by Goldfeld. In particular, it is assumed that in addition to the deposit variables acting as constraints on bank demand for assets, the flow of commercial loans is also a constraint and not a decision variable of the bank. This last assumption is based on the "customer" relationship that forces a bank to accept loan requests, at least in the short-run. The decision variable of the bank in the commercial loan part of the portfolio is the rate it charges to its customers. Under these assumptions it is the flow of loans that enters as an explanatory variable in the asset demand equations while the rate charged on these loans is excluded as a potential explanatory variable.

The primary security-holdings of commercial banks are Government bonds, state-local bonds (municipals), and mortgages. Commercial loans also make up a large portion of the portfolio, although we shall not estimate such a bank demand equation for reasons just cited. Banks also hold excess reserves and, as a liability, borrowings from the Federal Reserve System. We shall estimate demand equations for these also.

COMMERCIAL BANK DEMAND EQUATIONS

The additional notation that shall be employed in the estimated equations is as follows:

GB^c: Government bonds (of commercial banks)

GBS^c/GB^c: Short-term Governments as a ratio to total Governments

SL^c: State-local bonds (of commercial banks)

M^c: Mortgages (of commercial banks)

L^c: Commercial loans (of commercial banks)

[22] See [26].

B^c: Borrowings from the "Fed" (of commercial banks)

ER^c: Excess reserves (of commercial banks)

DD^c: Private demand deposits (of commercial banks)

TD^c: Private time deposits (of commercial banks)

$(D + T)^c_G$: Government (Federal and state-local) time deposits plus demand deposits (of commercial banks)

TXA: Tax accruals (of commercial banks)

i_{TB}: Treasury bill rate (3 months)

i_D: Federal Reserve discount rate

R^u: Unborrowed reserves of commercial banks (corrected for reserve requirement changes)

DT: Dummy variable, which has a value of 1 during periods of tight money and zero during easy money (text explains the construction of this variable)

Given the background information on commercial banks discussed in the previous section and the notation just presented, it is now appropriate to set forth the behavioral equations that were estimated for commercial banks. A complete discussion of each equation and the alternative specifications that were considered follows.

$$
\begin{aligned}
GB^c = \; & .628 \; DD^c + \; .675 \; (D + T)^c_G - \; .946 \; \Delta L^c \\
& (2.70) \qquad\quad (4.61) \qquad\qquad\qquad (4.75) \\
& - \; .579 \; DD^c_{-1} - \; .648 \; (D + T)^c_{G-1} + \; .936 \; GB^c_{-1} \\
& (2.97) \qquad\qquad (4.30) \qquad\qquad\qquad\quad (14.4) \\
& - \; 877.8 \; S_1 + 445.0 \; S_2 + 1619.5 \; S_3 - 1518.9 \\
& \quad (.35) \qquad\quad (.27) \qquad\quad (1.24) \qquad\quad (.15) \\
& R^2 = .85 \qquad\qquad SE/DV = .021 \\
& SE = 1394.0 \qquad\quad DW = 2.30
\end{aligned}
\tag{6}
$$

$$
\begin{aligned}
GBS^c/GB^c = \; & .027 \; i_{TB} - \; .009 \; i_{GB} - \; .003 \; \Delta M^c + .0006 \; TXA^c \\
& (2.17) \qquad\quad (.45) \qquad\quad (2.19) \qquad\qquad (1.86) \\
& + \; .95 \; (GBS^c/GB^c)_{-1} - \; .047 \; S_1 + \; .019 \; S_2 \\
& \quad (16.8) \qquad\qquad\qquad\qquad (3.54) \qquad\quad (1.26) \\
& + \; .013 \; S_3 - \; .051 \\
& \quad (1.02) \qquad\quad (1.40) \\
& R^2 = .88 \qquad\qquad SE/DV = .098 \\
& SE = .031 \qquad\qquad DW = 1.41
\end{aligned}
\tag{7}
$$

$$SL^c = \underset{(3.25)}{.077} \; TD^c + \underset{(1.73)}{.046} \; (D + T)^c_{G-1} + \underset{(8.05)}{.719} \; SL^c_{-1}$$
$$+ \underset{(2.83)}{268.7} \; S_1 + \underset{(1.64)}{160.6} \; S_2 + \underset{(1.49)}{142.6} \; S_3 - \underset{(4.01)}{1237.1} \qquad (8)$$
$$R^2 = .99 \qquad\qquad SE/DV = .024$$
$$SE = 260.1 \qquad\qquad DW = 2.01$$
$$RHO = .45$$

$$M^c = \underset{(.65)}{.014} \; DD^c + \underset{(3.65)}{.049} \; TD^c + \underset{(2.11)}{.123} \; \Delta L^c + \underset{(18.9)}{.873} \; M^c_{-1}$$
$$+ \underset{(.40)}{81.5} \; S_1 + \underset{(1.94)}{46.5} \; S_2 + \underset{(2.00)}{356.3} \; S_3 - \underset{(.47)}{969.0} \qquad (9)$$
$$R^2 = .99 \qquad\qquad SE/DV = .012$$
$$SE = 239.8 \qquad\qquad DW = 1.85$$

$$ER^c = \underset{(2.71)}{-52.0} \; i_{TB} + \underset{(1.93)}{.066} \; \Delta R^u + \underset{(3.58)}{.525} \; ER^c_{-1} - \underset{(1.32)}{57.0} \; S_1$$
$$- \underset{(1.39)}{45.0} \; S_2 - \underset{(.52)}{16.0} \; S_3 + \underset{(2.83)}{413.9} \qquad (10)$$
$$R^2 = .80 \qquad\qquad SE/DV = .101$$
$$SE = 53.0 \qquad\qquad DW = 1.72$$

$$B^c = \underset{(1.28)}{102.0} \; (i_{TB} - i_D) - \underset{(5.01)}{.405} \; \Delta R^u + \underset{(13.5)}{.771} \; B^c_{-1} - \underset{(4.32)}{472.0} \; S_1$$
$$- \underset{(1.99)}{133.0} \; S_2 - \underset{(2.52)}{167.0} \; S_3 + \underset{(6.24)}{368.0} \qquad (11)$$
$$R^2 = .88 \qquad\qquad SE/DV = .238$$
$$SE = 106.0 \qquad\qquad DW = 2.27$$

The demand for Government bonds is explained in Equation 6. We shall discuss, first, the general approach taken in the specification of all the bank equations using this one as a particular example. To account for the regulation regarding "pledged" assets, the deposit variable was broken into three instead of two (Goldfeld used DD and TD only) categories. The three groups are demand deposits of the private sector, time deposits of the private sector, and total deposits of the Federal and state-local governments. These three deposit variables were tried initially in every security demand equation. In Equation 6, only DD^c and $(D + T)^c_G$ were significant (TD^c had a t-value around .10). In order to test for the substitutability between assets, the own rate and various combinations of rates on alternative bank assets were included in each equation. In Equation 6, the rates that were entered had coefficients that were quite insignificant (t-values below .5) and often had the wrong signs. They do not, therefore, appear in the final version of Equation 6. The commercial loan variable was added to every equation as a constraint in accordance with our previous discussion. In Equation 6 it appears with a negative sign indicating that increased loan demand is financed, at least in the short-run, by selling Governments.

Let us now discuss the specific features of Equation 6 and describe the implications for bank portfolio behavior. Unlike Goldfeld, we have specified a demand equation for total Governments rather than a demand for "shorts" and a demand for "longs." This is not even considered for other intermediaries because their holdings of Governments in the under-one-year category are extremely small. Commercial banks, however, held (during the 1953–1965 period) an average of 30 percent of their Government bond portfolio in the "under-one" category; hence the maturity distribution should be explained. This is done in this model in Equation 7, which shall be discussed shortly.

In the test for substitutability between Governments and other bank assets just described, the own rate was tried in Equation 6 in several different forms, the long-term bond rate was used, the bill rate was used, and an average of the two was also tried (a simple average with weights of .5 to each rate was used, and, alternatively, a weighted average with weights of .7 for i_{GB} and .3 for i_{TB} was tried). The failure to reveal any substitutability between Governments and the rest of the portfolio is in agreement with the findings of Goldfeld. A partial explanation of this phenomenon will be discussed in the context of the review of overall bank portfolio behavior.

The constraint variables in the GB^c equation are DD^c, $(D + T)^c{}_G$ the lagged values of these variables, and ΔL^c. The fact that $DD^c{}_{-1}$ and $(D + T)^c{}_{G-1}$ enter the equation significantly implies that funds are put into Governments as a short-run repository after an increment to these two categories of deposits. A major portion of these funds does not remain in Governments for more than one period. A similar type of reaction was found for mutual savings banks. The difference is, of course, that there remains a net addition to GB^c in response to increases in DD^c and $(D + T)^c{}_G$ that was not true for MSB. The significant coefficient for the $(D + T)^c{}_G$ variable and the failure of TD^c to enter significantly reveals the importance of segmenting deposits into "private" and "public" components to account for the "pledging" regulations. The speed of adjustment in Equation 6 is slower than that of the previous set of equations and also slower than for the remaining bank behavioral equations. A little more than 6 percent of adjustment occurs within the first period, implying that about 25 percent of adjustment occurs after one year. These magnitudes are in rough agreement with the speeds of adjustment for

Governments in bank portfolios found by Goldfeld (taking city and country banks together).

The demand for short-term Governments relative to long-term Governments is expressed in Equation 7. The Treasury bill rate and the long-term bond rate appear in this equation (although the latter is quite insignificant), suggesting that there is some substitutability between "shorts" and "longs." An attempt was made to enter explicit proxies for expected future rates by including weighted averages of past values of i_{TB} and i_{GB}. These proxy variables did not prove significant. The two other variables in the equation (besides seasonals and the lagged dependent variable) reflect other portfolio effects that influence GBS^c/GB^c. The negative coefficient attached to ΔM^c implies that when mortgages are acquired the actual purchase is financed by selling short-term Governments that probably were accumulated (relative to "longs") in anticipation of the addition to mortgage holdings. By including the flow of another asset (that is, ΔM^c) as an explanatory variable, the implicit assumption being made is that the decision to change mortgage holdings is made prior to the "short" versus "long" decision in the Government bond portfolio. The positive coefficient attached to tax accruals indicates that holdings of short-term Governments (relative to "longs") are increased in expectation of having to liquidate asset holdings to pay the accruing taxes. The speed of adjustment in GBS^c/GB^c is rather slow; only 5 percent of the discrepancy between actual and desired holdings is eliminated in the first period.

Other variables were also tried in Equation 7. The deposit mix, that is, time deposits relative to demand deposits, did not prove to be significant. The loan variable was also tried on grounds similar to the use of ΔM^c. It also was quite insignificant. The results for this equation are still unsatisfactory. It is quite possible that the data used are too aggregative to yield meaningful behavioral results in this area. Because the precise form of this equation does not affect the workings of the other components and markets in the model (to be discussed in Chapter 4), the results of Equation 7 seem reasonable enough for a first approximation.

Equation 8 describes commercial bank demand for state-local bonds. As in the demand for Governments, there are no interest rate variables, implying zero substitutability between SL^c and other assets in the portfolio. The deposit variables in the equation are time deposits and total deposits of the government sector lagged one period. The significant coefficient (at the 5 percent level with a one-tailed test) attached to $(D + T)^c_{G-1}$ and the fact that DD^c was quite insignificant when it was tried in Equation 8 indicates once again the importance of separating public deposits from private deposits. The speed of adjustment in Equation 8 is rather quick, especially in comparison with the results reported by Goldfeld. Our results imply that 28 percent of adjustment occurs in the first period or over 70 percent is completed after one year. In contrast, Goldfeld's estimates imply an initial adjustment of only 2 percent.

The demand for mortgages, Equation 9, also does not have any interest rate variables. The insignificance of the relevant rates when they were tried confirms the independence-in-demand results gleaned from Equations 6 and 8. The deposit variables that are in the M^c demand equation, TD^c and DD^c, imply a number of reasonable behavioral patterns for commercial banks. First, a switch of funds from DD^c to TD^c increases mortgage demand. This is to be expected because the illiquidity of mortgages makes them a risky investment for demand deposit funds (this helps to explain, perhaps, the low t-value for DD^c). Second, the failure of $(D + T)^c_G$ to appear in Equation 9 (when it was included it had a t-value very close to zero) is quite reasonable because public deposits cannot be secured by mortgages. The positive coefficient attached to ΔL^c implies that not only are commercial loans not financed by mortgage sales but, in addition, the holdings of these two assets seem to move together.[23] The speed of adjustment implied by the M^c demand equation is that 13 percent occurs within the first quarter or that about 45 percent of adjustment is completed after one year.

Before discussing the excess reserves equation and the borrowing equation, let us examine the relationship between the security demand equations. The failure to find any substitute relationships between security demands, while in agreement with Goldfeld's conclusions, seems to go against the a priori profit (or utility) maximization objective assumed for financial intermediaries. Banks, however, are subject to a number of special forces that might explain this lack of portfolio response to interest rate changes. The strong customer relationship expressed in our use of ΔL^c as a constraint variable may very well force banks to readjust their portfolios irrespective (or in spite) of interest rate movements. The "pledging" requirement for public deposits makes the portfolio choice, say, between municipals (or Governments) and mortgages more dependent on relative deposit flows than on relevant interest rates. Similarly, the volume of time deposits relative to demand deposits seems to be a more important consideration than interest rates in determining mortgage flows. The same holds true for the choice between Governments versus state-local bonds; that is, Equation 8 has the TD^c variable and no DD^c variable whereas the reverse is true for Equation 6. Although the

---

[23] Goldfeld finds a similar comovement in long-term Governments held by country banks and commercial loans. See [22], p. 132. Although our results do not corroborate his, the point is that a positive sign for the ΔL^c variable in certain security demand equations is not inconceivable.

rationale for the TD^c-DD^c mix affecting these two security holdings is not very clear, it might be explained as follows: Because state-local bonds are much less marketable than Governments, when time deposits increase and demand deposits fall banks take the opportunity to increase SL^c and to decrease GB^c.

The constraint variables of Equations 6, 8, and 9 imply a rather consistent behavior pattern. The change in commercial loans is financed in the short-run primarily by selling off Governments. The long-run impact of a unit increase in TD^c raises SL^c by .28 and raises M^c by .39. The long-run impact of an increase in $(D + T)^c_G$ is to increase SL^c by approximately .18 and to increase GB^c by .5, the sum of which is not equal to unity (as one might expect) but is certainly within one standard error thereof. The long-run impact of a unit increase in demand deposits according to Equation 9 raises M^c by .1 and raises GB^c by .77. The remainder of DD^c and TD^c unaccounted for by our equations is probably used for commercial loans over and above the amounts indicated by the coefficients of the ΔL^c variables in our equations.

The dynamic response to a change in $(D + T)^c_G$ is suggested and confirmed by both Equation 6 and Equation 8. Initially, the increment goes into Governments. After one period a major portion of the addition to Governments is sold (signified by the negative coefficient attached to $(D + T)^c_{G-1}$ in Equation 6), and part of the proceeds are placed gradually into state-local bonds (indicated by the positive coefficient attached to $(D + T)^c_{G-1}$ in Equation 8).

We shall return to an overall evaluation of the commercial bank equations after having discussed the excess reserves and borrowing equations. Equation 10 describes banks' demand for excess reserves. In addition to including the Treasury bill rate (i_{TB}) as an explanatory variable, an open market variable has been added to the demand equation to reflect the direct influence of changes in reserves available to banks on the holdings of excess reserves. This is primarily a short-run reaction because an increment in unborrowed reserves is first held partly in cash (excess reserves) and is then used to purchase earning assets (or to reduce borrowings). The R^u variable is therefore entered in first-difference form (the level of R^u was not significant when tried). The negative sign attached to i_{TB} reflects the effect of increases in the opportunity cost of funds on demand for ER^c. The positive sign attached to ΔR^u implies, as was just suggested, that initially an increase in reserves is held partially (only 7 percent) as excess reserves and only after one period do these funds enter the market for securities or loans. The speed of adjustment for ER^c is rather quick, as one might expect; about 47 percent of adjustment occurs after one period, and 90 percent is completed within one year.

Borrowings from the "Fed" is described by Equation 11. The positive coefficient attached to $(i_{TB} - i_D)$ implies that increases in the bill rate relative to the discount rate encourage an increase in bank borrowing. This is the profit theory of borrowing. The reluctance aspect of borrowing is discussed briefly below. The insignificant coefficient attached to $(i_{TB} - i_D)$ suggests that the profit motive may, indeed, not be that strong. The negative sign attached to ΔR^u implies that increases in reserves reduce the incentive (and necessity) of banks to have liabilities at the "Fed." The speed of adjustment in Equation 11 is also fairly quick, although slower than ER^c. More than 20 percent of adjustment occurs after one quarter, and well over 60 percent of adjustment is completed after one year.

With regard to the reluctance influence on bank borrowing, much has already been done.[24] It has been shown that by entering a squared $(i_{TB} - i_D)$ variable into the borrowing equation, one accounts for the reluctance-surveillance effects on B^c.[25] The expected sign of $(i_{TB} - i_D)^2$ is negative. It has also been shown that it is necessary to distinguish between periods of easy money (when there is no surveillance) and tight money (when reluctance and surveillance ought to be strongest).[26] Accordingly, the $(i_{TB} - i_D)^2$ variable is multiplied by a dummy variable (DT), which has a value of 1 in tight-money periods and zero in easy-money periods. Between 1953 and 1965, DT has a value of zero during all of 1954, the first two quarters of 1958, and the first two quarters of 1961.[27] When $(i_{TB} - i_D)^2 (DT)$ was added to Equation 11, the t-value of $(i_{TB} - i_D)$ became even smaller and the coefficient was slightly negative. Hence, Equation 11 was reestimated with $(i_{TB} - i_D)^2 (DT)$ replacing $(i_{TB} - i_D)$. The results are as follows:

$$B^c = -308.0 \ (i_{TB} - i_D)^2 \ (DT) - .472 \ \Delta R^u + .808 \ B^c_{-1}$$
$$ (2.30) (8.30) (15.8)$$
$$ - \ 580.8 \ S_1 - 190.0 \ S_2 - 216.2 \ S_3 + 409.3$$
$$ (7.93) (3.96) (4.13) (7.49)$$
$$R^2 = .88 SE/DV = .234$$
$$SE = 102.7 DW = 2.46$$

(11a)

Equation 11a suggests that reluctance does play a role in influencing bank borrowing. Because the interaction between the profit motive and the reluctance effect is still unclear we shall use Equation 11 primarily

[24] See [41], [42], and [23].
[25] See [41].
[26] See [42].
[27] See *ibid.* for an explanation of how easy and tight money are designated.

as the representative borrowing equation of our model. It is not our purpose here to examine in detail the profit-versus-reluctance impacts on bank borrowing. The extent to which increases in i_D reduce borrowing *ceteris paribus* is the major reason for our overall concern with bank borrowing. Its importance will become clear in the calculation of the reduced form in Chapter 5. Because Equation 11 presents this effect of i_D on B^c most clearly, we shall use it as part of our model.

The bank borrowing equation was estimated from 1954 through 1965. The reason for omitting 1953 is that the excess profits tax of the Korean War was still in effect. Rather than using a dummy variable to account for the changed incentive to borrow during this period, it seemed less of a problem to eliminate the four observations in question. All of the other bank equations were estimated over the normal 1953–1965 period.

The overall performance of the behavioral equations for commercial banks is quite good. The high R^2's, the low ratios of standard error to the mean of the dependent variable (except for the B^c equation), and the lack of significant serial correlation (except for the SL^c equation where the autoregressive structure had to be estimated) all suggest that the estimated equations are close approximations to real-world behavior. The revelation that banks do not adjust their security portfolio in response to interest rate changes has been explained as resulting from the myriad of other influences on portfolio composition. The only areas in which relative interest rates seem to play a role are in the determination of the maturity structure of Government bond holdings and in the demands for cash items, that is, excess reserves and borrowings. The sensitivity of B^c and ER^c to the bill rate will be important for the impact of monetary policy on the entire model. It is the same as having an interest-sensitive money supply function in the model.[28] Another result indicating that our estimated equations are quite reasonable is the quick speed of adjustment in the regressions, especially in contrast with the results of previous models.

PENSION PLANS

AN INTRODUCTION

Corporate and state-local government retirement funds are among the fastest growing components of the financial sector of the economy.[29] Before discussing the basic characteristics of pension funds, let us look

---

[28] See [22], pp. 190–192.
[29] For a complete analysis of pension plan behavior, see in [10], Research Study Three, "Noninsured Corporate and State and Local Government Retirement Funds in the Financial Structure" by Victor L. Andrews, pp. 381–520.

at the percentage distribution of asset holdings of pension plans at the end of 1960 in order to help decide the relevant interest rates to use in our demand equations. Corporate pension plans held 7.1 percent of assets in Government bonds, 49.2 percent in corporate bonds, 33.1 percent in common stock, and the residual was divided between cash, mortgages, and other assets.[30] State-local plans held 31.9 percent of assets in Government bonds, 23.7 percent in state-local bonds, 33.0 percent in corporate bonds, 2.2 percent in corporate stock, and the rest was divided between cash, mortgages, and other assets.[31] Demand equations will be specified only for corporate bonds and Government bonds. We chose not to estimate demand equations for equities and municipals for a number of reasons. The data on holdings of equities is extremely poor. The wide fluctuation in the market value of corporate stock makes the variability in the holdings of equities a function primarily of changes in the stock-price level rather than in portfolio decision making. An attempt will be made, however, to examine the responses of corporate bond and Government bond demands to changes in the price level. A demand equation for state-local bonds was not attempted because there is no "maximization" decision involved in pension plan holdings of municipals because the income of all pension plans is tax free. This becomes clear when one recognizes that corporate pension plans, in fact, do not hold state-local securities. The state-local funds' holdings of municipals are most likely the result of nonprice influences.

In contrast with the three deposit institutions already analyzed, pension plans are almost completely exempt from unforeseeable demands for cash outflows. Benefit payments are the only significant outflow of cash, and they are actuarially predictable.[32] Given this type of built-in liquidity, there probably will not be any flow variables acting as constraints such as was found for GB^u and GB^c. The demand equations will be specified as before, and we shall, once again, try both linear and ratio formulations of the demand functions.

PENSION PLAN DEMAND EQUATIONS

The new notation that will be used is as follows:

GB^p: Government bonds (of pension plans)

CB^p: Corporate bonds (of pension plans)

A^p: Assets (of pension plans)

---

[30] See [10], p. 521.

[31] *Ibid.*, p. 529.

[32] *Ibid.*, p. 423.

The final estimated demand equations for GB^p and CB^p are:

$$GB^p = 295.1\ i_{GB} - 255.2\ i_{CB} + .003\ A^p + .733\ GB^p_{-1}$$
$$(2.52)(3.21)(1.10)(8.64)$$
$$+ 72.4\ S_1 - 91.2\ S_2 - 45.6\ S_3 + 809.9$$
$$(1.90)(2.34)(1.19)(2.68)$$
$$R^2 = .94SE/DV = .033$$
$$SE = 96.8DW = 2.09$$

(12)

$$CB^p/A^p = .038\ i_{CB} - .057\ i_{GB} + .744\ (CB^p/A^p)_{-1}$$
$$(2.07)(2.30)(6.54)$$
$$- .003\ S_1 + .001\ S_2 + .002\ S_3 + .141$$
$$(1.32)(.41)(1.06)(1.85)$$
$$R^2 = .88SE/DV = .05$$
$$SE = .008DW = 1.77$$
$$RHO = .66$$

(13)

Equation 12, the demand for Governments, implies that Government bonds and corporate bonds are substitutes for each other in pension plan portfolios. The constraint variable A^p has a positive coefficient, but its t-value is low. This is indicative of the fact that Governments are not a "preferred investing asset" in pension plan portfolios. Higher yielding corporate bonds of good quality are used as the major investment in fixed income securities. The speed of adjustment implied by the coefficient of GB^p_{-1} is that 27 percent occurs within one period and that over 70 percent is completed after one year.

The demand for corporate bonds, Equation 13, is in ratio form rather than linear. The linear specification of the demand for CB^p produced an infinite speed of adjustment, and the estimated coefficients were quite insignificant. The reverse was true in the demand equations for GB^p. Equation 12 has a reasonable speed of adjustment whereas the ratio version of Government bond demand had an infinite speed of adjustment. It seems clear that for GB^p the linear form is the best approximation to reality, whereas for CB^p the ratio specification is most appropriate.

The demand equation for CB^p confirms the good substitute relationship between corporates and Governments in pension plan portfolios. The coefficient of the lagged dependent variable implies approximately the same speed of adjustment for CB^p as was revealed by Equation 12 for GB^p. The value of RHO recorded beneath Equation 13 ($RHO = .66$) reveals that without taking account of the autoregressive structure in the equation for CB^p, there would have been a serial correlation problem. The original equation, in fact, had a DW statistic equal to .73. As in most cases of autocorrelation, the probable cause is that some significant variables were left out of the regression equation. Accordingly, the original (pre-RHO) Equation 13 was amended to include the rate of change in the stock price level (Standard and Poor's average price level for 500 stocks). Presumably, pension plans determine, in part, their allocation of funds between equities and corporate bonds based upon capital gains potential of equities relative to the interest rate on bonds. When the rate of change in the stock price variable was added to the "pre-RHO" Equation 13, the DW statistic increased from .73 to 1.12. The latter still indicates the presence of autocorrelation, but less so than before. The rate of change in the stock price variable was significantly negative. All other variables in the equation remained essentially unchanged. When the autoregressive transformation was applied to the equation with the stock price variable, however, that variable became quite insignificant (t-value less than .5). Other specifications were also tried, for example, using different lagged values of the stock price average, or the GNP deflator or the dividend yield, each of which produced similar results; that is, the additional variable reduced the autocorrelation in part, but significant serial correlation still remained. Furthermore, when the autogressive transformation was applied, the newly added variables became very insignificant, just as with the stock price variable. It was decided to use the specification reported in Equation 13 based on the fact that the post-RHO equation was to be used in any case, and in that form of the final equation the stock price variable was quite insignificant.

The overall performance of the equations describing pension plan behavior is quite good. High R^2's, low standard errors relative to the mean of the dependent variable, and absence of serial correlation suggest that the final equations are reasonable approximations to reality. The Brainard–Tobin test regarding the sum of all interest rate responses equalling zero is not relevant here because the demand for a somewhat significant portion of the portfolio has not been estimated, that is, corporate equities. The long-run equilibrium response to an increase in assets should be, however, significantly less than unity so that the remainder of the portfolio not treated here will increase implicitly as A^p rises. A unit increase in A^p causes GB^p to rise by .01 in long-run equilibrium and causes CB^p to rise by .54 in the long run. This leaves over 45 percent of an increment to total assets to equities (and municipals). During the period covered by the estimated equations, the increment to equities relative to total assets varied between 30 and 55 percent, so that our estimated coefficients do seem to be of the correct order of magnitude.

LIFE INSURANCE COMPANIES

AN INTRODUCTION

In 1959, the percentage distribution of funds in the investment portfolio of insurance companies was Government bonds, 6.0 (percent); mortgages, 34.5; corporate bonds, 39.9; corporate stock, 4.0; other assets, 15.6.[33] We shall specify demand equations for Governments, corporate bonds, and mortgages, with the long-term interest rates on these three assets serving as explanatory variables in the equations.

One important result stemming from the actuarially predictable nature of the liabilities of life insurance companies (LIC) is the use of the forward commitment process in allocating funds among alternative assets.[34] The relative stability of the cash flow available for investment enables life insurance companies to form a binding agreement to lend a specified amount of money at a given rate of interest for a certain number of years, within an agreed-upon time period. The desire to maintain a fully invested position encourages the use of the forward-commitment process. Because the forward commitment of funds is used mainly in investment in corporate bonds and mortgages, the initial specification of the demand equations should incorporate some measure of the impact of forward commitments on current holdings of these assets. It might have been more desirable to explain the determinants of the forward commitment of funds to alternative assets. Initial attempts at estimating such equations were not successful.

As in the case of pension plans, the fact that corporate stocks present (to some extent) a feasible investment opportunity suggests the use of some measure of stock-price levels in the demand equations for other assets. As an alternative to the level of stock prices, we shall also try the GNP deflator (as was done for pension plans). Either of these price level variables should help explain the portfolio response to the "inflation threat." It should be noted that the deposit-type financial intermediaries (especially SLA and commercial banks) do not have this opportunity to hedge against inflation. It is for this reason that price levels did not show up (although tried) in their security demand equations.

LIFE INSURANCE COMPANY DEMAND EQUATIONS

The demand equations for Government bonds, corporate bonds, and mortgages by life insurance companies use the following additional notation.

---

[33] *Ibid.*, p. 41.
[34] See [37], pp. 185–191.

GB^l: Government bonds (of life insurance companies)
CB^l: Corporate bonds (of life insurance companies)
M^l: Mortgages (of life insurance companies)
A^l: Assets (of life insurance companies)
CM^l: Commitments to mortgages (of life insurance companies)
L/V: Loan-to-value ratio on mortgages
$\Delta P/P$: Rate of change in the GNP deflator

The estimated demand equations are as follows:

$$GB^l = 65.6\ i_{GB} - 1647.8\ \Delta P/P + .429\ \Delta A^l - .016\ A^l$$
$$\qquad (.83) \qquad (2.72) \qquad\qquad (3.10) \qquad\quad (3.83)$$
$$+ .818\ GB^l_{-1} + 293.2\ S_1 + 229.6\ S_2$$
$$\quad (16.4) \qquad\quad (4.71) \qquad (3.49)$$
$$+ 266.7\ S_3 + 1968.7$$
$$\quad (5.08) \qquad (2.73)$$
$$R^2 = .99 \qquad\qquad SE/DV = .016$$
$$SE = 116.4 \qquad\qquad DW = 1.67$$

$$(14)$$

$$CB^l = 583.9\ i_{CB} - 331.6\ i_{GB} - 438.3\ i_M - 433.1\ \Delta P/P$$
$$\quad (2.18) \qquad\quad (1.69) \qquad\quad (1.60) \qquad\quad (.64)$$
$$+ .034\ A^l + .919\ CB^l_{-1} - 74.7\ S_1$$
$$\quad (1.59) \qquad\quad (15.0) \qquad\quad (1.22)$$
$$- 31.6\ S_2 - 164.3\ S_3 + 1612.9$$
$$\quad (.60) \qquad (3.10) \qquad\quad (2.66)$$
$$R^2 = .99 \qquad\qquad SE/DV = .003$$
$$SE = 129.3 \qquad\qquad DW = 1.68$$

$$(15)$$

$$M^l = -292.5\ (i_{CB} - i_M) + 240.1\ (i_{GB} - i_M) - 61.7\ L/V$$
$$\quad (1.26) \qquad\qquad\quad (1.37) \qquad\qquad\quad (1.68)$$
$$+ .059\ A^l + .541\ CM^l_{-2} + .891\ M^l_{-1} + 281.6$$
$$\quad (2.00) \qquad (3.17) \qquad\qquad (15.3) \qquad\quad (1.42)$$
$$R^2 = .99 \qquad\qquad SE/DV = .005$$
$$SE = 181.1 \qquad\qquad DW = 2.37$$

$$(16)$$

Equation 14 is the demand for Government bonds by life insurance companies. The only interest rate variable that appears here is i_{GB}, which has a rather low t-value. When other rates were included, all the t-values were less than .5 and some of the signs were incorrect. The rate of change in the GNP deflator, $\Delta P/P$, has a significant negative coefficient. The stock price level was also tried, and it too had a negative coefficient but was less significant than $\Delta P/P$. The significance of $\Delta P/P$ implies that LIC do adjust their portfolios in response to the threat of inflation; that is, they sell Governments and buy (perhaps) equities. The assets of LIC enter Equation 14 both as a level and as a first difference, similar to what was found for MSB demand for Governments. The positive coefficient for ΔA^l implies that initially an increment to assets is put into GB^l and after one period the funds are taken out and put elsewhere in the portfolio. The importance of a flow variable in LIC demands is surprising in light of the predictability of cash flows. This point was also made explicit with pension plans. The only explanation that can be given relates to the forward commitment process, and this will be discussed later. The negative sign for the level A^l suggests that governments are an "inferior asset" over the time period that is covered. Just as in the case of mutual savings banks, the excess holdings of Government bonds at the end of World War II were sold off gradually until the present. This continued decumulation of GB^l coupled with rapid increase in A^l over the same period explain the negative coefficient for total assets. The speed of adjustment implied by GB^l_{-1} in Equation 14 is that about 18 percent of adjustment occurs after one period or that about 55 percent of total adjustment is completed after one year.

The demand for corporate bonds (Equation 15) suggests that corporates are substitutes both for Governments and mortgages in LIC portfolios (i_{GB} and i_M are significant, or nearly so, at the 5 percent level using a one-tailed test). The $\Delta P/P$ variable enters here also with a negative sign, but it is not nearly significant. The total asset variable has a positive sign and is almost significant at the 5 percent level with a one-tailed test. The speed of adjustment for CB^l is about 8 percent during the first period, or close to 30 percent of adjustment is completed after one year.

The mortgage demand equation (Equation 16) was estimated by ordinary least squares. The TSLS version was distinctly inferior to Equation 16 in terms of poorer agreement with a priori signs of the coefficients, lower t-values, a slower speed of adjustment, and greater serial correlation. The signs of the interest rate differentials of Equation 16 suggest that mortgages are substitutes for corporates and are complements with Governments. (Note that the implicit sign of i_M is positive as is required.) Although the t-values of the rate differentials are significant only at the 10 percent level (using a one-tailed test), they were included in the final version of M^l demand reported here for a number of reasons. First, the substitute relationship between mortgages and corporates is now symmetrical. Second, although the complementarity between mortgages and Governments is not symmetrical, when that term ($i_{GB} - i_M$) was suppressed the mortgage rate and the corporate bond rate became quite insignificant. Finally, when all rates were excluded from the equation, the speed of adjustment of the equation became infinite. The loan-to-value ratio on mortgages (L/V) enters Equation 16 with a negative sign, that is, the higher the L/V ratio the less willing are insurance companies to hold a mortgage. This variable was tried in the mortgage demand equations of other financial intermediaries, but it never was significant. The mortgage commitment variable (CM) appears with the expected positive coefficient and is lagged two periods. This is the lag that produced the largest t-value for CM. The total assets of LIC is the relevant constraint variable and is significant. The speed of adjustment in M^l demand is 11 percent during the first period, and over 35 percent of adjustment is completed after one year.

The consistency tests regarding the set of LIC portfolio equations suggest that the estimated equations do not imply contradictory behavioral patterns. Although there is a significant portion of assets whose demands are not explained and hence are viewed as a residual (yet this is much less than the "residual" in the portfolios of pension plans), the Brainard–Tobin tests can still be conducted. The sum of the responses of GB^l, CB^l, and M^l to a unit change in i_{GB} is minus \$27 million; the sum of the responses to a unit change in i_{CB} is \$291 million; and the sum of the responses to a unit change in i_M is \$386 million. The net responses are close enough to zero given the imperfect applicability of this test (see the initial discussion under mutual savings banks above), suggesting that the portfolio equations for LIC do not violate the Brainard–Tobin conditions (at least initially). The long-run response to a unit change in A^l should be less than unity. The actual reactions as implied by Equations 14 through 16 are a unit increment to A^l causes M^l to rise by .55, CB^l rises by .32 while GB^l falls by .09. The sum of these long-run responses is .78. This is within the acceptable range.

There is one inconsistency in the dynamics of adjustment that was also found for mutual savings banks. The GB^l demand equation has the change in total assets as an explanatory variable, yet neither the CB^l nor the M^l equation has a ΔA^l variable (it would have to be opposite in sign). An increment to assets goes into GB^l first, and then, after one period, the Governments are sold and presumably other assets are purchased. As with MSB, although CB^l and M^l continue to increase during the second period, the magnitudes involved still suggest a discrepancy between decreases in GB^l in the second period and the increments to CB^l and M^l. The "residual" assets of the portfolio, especially equities, can account for part of the remaining difference. In addition, the lagged mortgage commitment variable (and its implications for cash holdings) in the M^l demand equation can probably make up the remaining discrepancy. There is likely to be an addition to cash balances prior to executing the mortgage commitment so that the cash portion of residual assets is very likely to increase when the holdings of Governments are sold after the first period.

The overall performance of the demand equations for LIC signified by the high R^2's, the low standard errors, and the absence of serial correlation suggest that the regressions present an accurate picture of LIC portfolio behavior. The substitute-complement relationships that were revealed agree with a priori expectations that portfolio allocation by financial intermediaries responds to interest rate changes.

OTHER INSURANCE COMPANIES

AN INTRODUCTION

The category called other insurance companies (OIC) in the Flow of Funds data refers to all insurance companies besides life insurance companies. The most inclusive category of "other insurance" is property and casualty insurance. Although there are differences between property insurance companies and casualty insurance companies, they are frequently discussed and analyzed under one heading.[35] The importance of "other insurance" in finance is obvious from the fact that assets of non-life insurance companies have grown from 400 million in 1898 to 29 billion in 1960.[36] The composition of the $29 billion portfolio at the end of 1960 was Government bonds, 5.5 billion; state-local bonds, 7.6 billion; corporate stocks, 9.3 billion; and the remainder divided between cash and small amounts of other bonds.[37] The two assets for which we shall specify demand equations are Governments and municipals. A demand equation for equities shall not be estimated for reasons cited above in connection with pension plans.

Unlike life insurance companies, the liabilities of property and casualty insurance companies cannot be predicted with precise accuracy because of the shorter duration of the insurance contract and the ever present danger of catastrophe causing a drain on the assets of a company.[38] This variability in liability flow makes it likely that the change in total assets will appear as an explanatory variable in the demand equations. The shorter duration of the insurance contract also does not permit OIC to use the forward commitment process as do life insurance companies.

[35] See [2].
[36] *Ibid.*, p. 23.
[37] *Ibid.*, p. 50.
[38] *Ibid.*, pp. 34 and 54.

The legal status of property and casualty insurance companies also influences their investment policies. Because the earnings of these insurance companies are fully liable to the corporation income tax and because equities are legal investments, we find a distinct tendency for "non-life" companies to concentrate their investments in tax-exempt municipals and corporate stock (which receives the favorable capital gains treatment).[39]

OTHER INSURANCE COMPANY DEMAND EQUATIONS

The additional notation that shall be used in the OIC demand equations is

GB^o: Government bonds (of other insurance companies)

SL^o: State-local bonds (of other insurance companies)

A^o: Assets (of other insurance companies)

$\Delta SPL/SPL$: Rate of change in the stock price level (Standard and Poor's)

The estimated equations for other insurance companies are as follows:

$$
\begin{aligned}
GB^o = {}& 394.7\ i_{GB} - 348.1\ i_{SL} + .102\ \Delta A^o - .014\ A^o \\
& \quad (4.16) \qquad (3.96) \qquad (2.98) \qquad\quad (3.54) \\
& + .913\ GB^o_{-1} - 194.2\ S_1 - 148.1\ S_2 \\
& \quad (15.9) \qquad\quad (7.98) \qquad (6.17) \\
& - 12.7\ S_3 + 487.7 \\
& \quad (.54) \qquad (1.22) \\
& R^2 = .94 \qquad\quad SE/DV = .01 \\
& SE = 59.2 \qquad\quad DW = 1.64
\end{aligned}
\tag{17}
$$

$$
\begin{aligned}
SL^o/A^o = {}& .004\ i_{SL} - .005\ i_{GB} - .021\ \Delta SPL/SPL \\
& \quad (2.23) \qquad (2.45) \qquad (3.77) \\
& + .965\ (SL^o/A^o)_{-1} + .002\ S_1 \\
& \quad (69.2) \qquad\qquad\quad (1.83) \\
& + .001\ S_2 - .003\ S_3 + .017 \\
& \quad (.58) \qquad (.32) \qquad (6.46) \\
& R^2 = .99 \qquad\quad SE/DV = .009 \\
& SE = .0023 \qquad DW = 1.05
\end{aligned}
\tag{18}
$$

[39] *Ibid.*, pp. 43, 48, and 53.

The demand for Governments (Equation 17) suggests that state-local bonds and Government bonds are good substitutes for each other in OIC portfolios. The demand for GB^o is also related to both the level of total assets and the change in assets, as was true of the demand for Governments by MSB and LIC. As with these two other intermediaries, the flow variable has a positive coefficient and the stock variable has a negative coefficient. The negative coefficient attached to A^o cannot be explained, as was done in the case of MSB and LIC, by the large (disequilibrium) stock of Governments held at the end of World War II. We note without further explanation that since 1953 the holdings of Governments by OIC have remained fairly constant or have decreased slightly, whereas assets have been increasing at an extremely rapid pace. This indicates that Governments may be considered an "inferior asset" by OIC (as was also suggested for MSB and LIC). The positive coefficient for ΔA^o implies that there is an initial placement of funds into Governments when an increment to assets occurs, and after one period there is a shift to other assets in the portfolio. The speed of adjustment in the demand for GB^o is slightly less than 9 percent during the first period, whereas a little more than 30 percent is completed after one year.

Equation 18, the demand for state-local bonds by OIC, is in ratio form. The linear specification of SL^o demand resulted in an infinite speed of adjustment (same as the ratio specification of Equation 17). The coefficients of i_{GB} and i_{SL} confirm the substitute relationship between Governments and state-local bonds revealed in the GB^o demand equation. The rate of change in the stock price level appears with a significant negative coefficient, implying that the demand for state-local bonds falls as actual capital gains on equities increase (presumably there is a corresponding increase in demand for equities). The speed of adjustment in SL^o demand is 3.5 percent in the first period, or less than 15 percent of adjustment is completed after one year.

The overall performance of the demand equations for other insurance companies is good except for the serial correlation that exists in the final version of Equation 18. Other variables were tried in the SL^o demand equation, such as ΔA^o and lagged values of the other explanatory variables, but none of them succeeded in eliminating the autocorrelation. When the autoregressive structure was estimated and the reported equation was reestimated using the calculated value of RHO, the signs of all the variables remained unchanged but the t-values of i_{SL} and i_{GB} were reduced substantially. Because the substitutability between Governments and municipals was confirmed by the GB^o demand equation as well as the reported SL^o demand, it was decided to use Equation 18 as just recorded despite the serial correlation.

The consistency tests of Brainard and Tobin are, as in the case of pension plans, of highly doubtful applicability because a large portion of OIC assets have been relegated to the "residual" (that is, corporate stock makes up the bulk of this category). The long-run equilibrium response of GB^o and SL^o demand to an increment in assets should, therefore, be significantly less than unity. A unit increase in A^o causes an equilibrium response in SL^o of $+.49$ and a response of $-.16$ in GB^o. The remainder of A^o is available for other assets (equities in particular).

SECURITY DEMAND EQUATIONS

SOME CONCLUSIONS

The security demand equations reported in this chapter describe the portfolio behavior of six financial intermediaries (MSB, SLA, commercial banks, pension plans, LIC, and OIC) with respect to four financial market instruments, Government bonds, corporate bonds, mortgages, and municipals. The major implications of the estimated demand equations are summarized below. Four of the six financial institutions do respond to changes in relative interest rates in their allocation of investment funds; they are mutual savings banks, pension plans, life insurance companies, and property and casualty insurance companies. Commercial banks and savings and loan associations do not seem to react to relative interest rates in the determination of portfolio allocation. Other factors, such as deposit composition for banks and the overwhelming objective of home-loan financing for SLA, are the prime determinants of the portfolio mix.

The two securities that are closest substitutes for each other (in the portfolios that hold both) are Government bonds and corporate bonds. Mortgages and corporate bonds also seem to be substitutes (especially for LIC). There is some evidence (from MSB and LIC equations) that mortgages and Governments are complementary in demand. State-local bonds and Government bonds are independent in demand for commercial banks, whereas they seem to be substitutes for property and casualty insurance companies. All of these substitute-complement relationships are in agreement with the a priori expectations set forth in Chapter 2. There is no conclusive evidence on the actual relationship between mortgages and state-local bonds or between corporates and state-local bonds. In fact, the only institution holding significant amounts of these two combinations is commercial banks. It would not be correct to draw the "independence-in-demand" conclusion for these two sets of securities in general, because banks do not seem to be influenced at all by relative interest rates.

There were a number of tests that were used to check the internal consistency of the set of demand equations. The general conclusion is that the reported equations do not violate the basic requirements of a financial model. In using these consistency checks, an attempt was being made to judge the reliability of each equation not only with regard to its individual statistical characteristics (R^2's and so on) but also as to how well each equation fits into the model. Another important result that lends credibility to the behavioral equations is the relatively quick speeds of adjustment that have been estimated. As was indicated before, most previous studies of the financial sector have found unreasonably slow adjustment of actual holdings to desired holdings.

Chapter 4

ESTIMATION OF A COMPLETE ECONOMETRIC MODEL

ADDITIONAL BEHAVIORAL EQUATIONS: THE REQUIREMENTS

The security demand equations presented in the last chapter comprise just one segment of an entire econometric model. Security supply equations and equilibrium conditions (or explicit interest-rate equations) must be introduced so that market rates are determined as endogenous variables. Furthermore, the constraint variables in the demand equations, for example, the liabilities of financial intermediaries and commercial loans, should be endogenous variables also in a model of behavior in the financial sector. Demand equations by the public for the liabilities of financial institutions and commercial loans will, therefore, be specified. The interest rates on liabilities of financial intermediaries are determined either endogenously through the introduction of an "interest-rate-offered" function (instead of a simple quantity-supplied function) or are assumed to be given exogenously.

The specifications of security supply equations and the demand equations for financial intermediary liabilities result in the introduction of national income variables (for example, GNP and investment) into our model. We shall specify consumption and investment functions and define national income in order to account for the endogenous nature of these variables. The market for bank reserves will be completed through the introduction of Federal Reserve policy variables and an equilibrium condition in the reserves market. This market will prove to be one of the central segments of the entire model.

It is also worth mentioning at this point that there are three assets in the model whose yields are legally set equal to zero, namely the rates of interest on demand deposits, bank reserves, and currency. These restrictions mean that three potential relationships must be dropped from the model; financial supplies and demands must reach balance, with three fewer elements to vary than in a more general system. We shall point out the potential equations that will not be included in this model during our discussions of the various sectors. A thorough analysis of the way in which the system operates shall be deferred until the specification and estimation of the set of remaining equations just described is completed. This short discussion is meant to outline the rationale for proceeding to specify these equations and the need for including them in our system. It is also worth noting that these steps are prerequisites for a formal analysis of the implications of our demand relationships for monetary policy and the impact of policy on portfolio behavior. Because these remaining equations are not the focal point of this study, we shall rely heavily on the work of other authors who have specialized in the various subsectors. In certain appropriate situations the actual equations estimated by other "model-builders" shall be used.

SECURITY-SUPPLY EQUATIONS

The following securities appear in the model: Government bonds, state-local bonds, corporate bonds, and mortgages. The supplies of Governments and municipals are assumed to be exogenously determined. Although these assumptions are also made in the Goldfeld and De Leeuw models, we must point out that it might be more appropriate to treat the supplies of these securities as endogenous. Until correct "policy equations" can be specified, we must simplify the system by making these variables exogenous.

The supply equations for mortgages and corporate bonds are specified with the following new notation.

$\overline{CB}$: Corporate bonds outstanding

I^c: Corporate investment in plant and equipment

RD: Retained earnings plus depreciation

$\overline{M}$: Mortgages outstanding

Y^d: Disposable income

ΔHH: Household formation

The estimated supply equations are as follows:

$$\overline{CB} = .366\ I^c - .252\ RD_{-1} + .98\ \overline{CB}_{-1} + 282.3\ S_1$$
$$\quad (4.33)\qquad (4.12)\qquad\quad (126.7)\qquad\quad (1.40)$$
$$-\ 182.3\ S_2 - 15.2\ S_3 + 1229.7$$
$$\quad (1.32)\qquad (.11)\qquad (4.67)$$
$$R^2 = .99 \qquad\qquad SE/DV = .005$$
$$SE = 333.5 \qquad\qquad DW = 2.28 \tag{19}$$

$$\Delta \overline{M} = -2287.7\ \Delta i_M + .009\ \Delta Y^d + .777\ \Delta HH$$
$$\qquad (2.55)\qquad\quad (1.80)\qquad\quad (.57)$$
$$+\ .820\ \Delta \overline{M}_{-1} - 572.3\ S_1 + 945.7\ S_2$$
$$\quad (8.73)\qquad\quad (3.30)\qquad\quad (4.58)$$
$$R^2 = .90 \qquad SE/DV = .116$$
$$SE = 487.4 \qquad DW = 2.61 \tag{20}$$

The supply of corporate bonds (Equation 19) is positively related to corporate investment and negatively related to internally generated funds lagged one period, RD_{-1}. The lagged dependent variable enters with a positive coefficient suggesting, as would be expected, that not only does the current level of investment affect current corporate bonds outstanding but also a weighted average of past values of I^c affects $\overline{CB}$. Similarly, a weighted average of past values of RD also affects current $\overline{CB}$. Conspicuous by their absence are the corporate bond rate and other market rates. It was expected that higher levels of i_{CB} would reduce $\overline{CB}$. In the trial investigations of Equation 19 the corporate bond rate was tried in numerous configurations, for example, lagged values, first differences, and explicit weighted averages of past values, none of which produced negative coefficients for i_{CB} with any degree of significance.[1]

The mortgage supply equation (Equation 20) is presented in first-difference form rather than as levels. The "levels-version" of Equation 20 contained a serious multicollinearity problem so that first-differences were tried.[2] The constant term in the first-difference equation drops out by simple subtraction. It was tried, nevertheless, representing a time

[1] See [3] for a comprehensive examination of corporate bond supply equations.
[2] See [47] for a general discussion of the mortgage supply equation. The specification presented here differs slightly from the one there, but the general approach is the same.

variable in a preliminary version of Equation 20 along with the "seasonals." The constant term does not appear in the $\overline{M}$ equation that is reported here (only two "seasonals" are included) because it was not significant when the household formation variable (ΔHH) was entered as an explanatory variable. Although the ΔHH variable is not significant in Equation 20, it was retained because on a priori grounds it should be in there explicitly rather than included in the constant. Just as increases in household formation should increase $\overline{M}$, so ought increases in some measure of income increase $\overline{M}$. The positive coefficient attached to Y^d in Equation 20 supports this hypothesis. Other measures of income were tried (for example, GNP), and so was wealth, but Y^d proved to be most significant. The negative coefficient attached to i_M suggests that an increase in the cost of mortgage funds reduces the supply, as would be expected. As in Equation 19, the significant coefficient attached to the lagged dependent variable in Equation 20 suggests that past values of the other explanatory variables affect current $\overline{M}$. Other variables that were tried in the $\overline{M}$ supply equation but that were not significant were the length of amortization on mortgages, the rent component of the consumer price index relative to the consumer price index, and corporate investment (to account for that portion of total mortgages used to finance industrial plant expenditure).

Residential construction does not appear in the mortgage supply equation because mortgages outstanding are viewed as a function of credit terms (i_M, and so on) and the desired level of housing stock. The latter is a function of income and household formation. In this respect the $\overline{M}$ equation differs from the corporate bond equation; that is, in the $\overline{CB}$ supply equation actual investment is included as an explanatory variable. One disturbing feature of the corporate bond equation is the extremely slow speed of adjustment implied by the coefficient of $\overline{CB}_{-1}$. This may be the result of the failure to decompose the determinants of the desired level of investment in Equation 19 as was done for residential construction in Equation 20. Attempts were made at doing so, but they resulted in equations that were inferior to the reported $\overline{CB}$ regression. It seems clear that additional intensive work in the security supply area may be a very fruitful topic for additional research.

DEMAND FOR FINANCIAL ASSETS

The liabilities of financial institutions are financial assets in the portfolio of the public. The demand equations in Chapter 3 used the stocks and/or flows of these liabilities as constraints on the portfolio demands of the financial intermediaries. Although we have assumed that the levels of these liabilities are taken as a constraint by the intermediaries, they ought to be endogenous variables in the entire model. There are seven of these financial assets: liabilities of life insurance companies, liabilities of pension plans, liabilities of property and casualty insurance companies, deposits at mutual savings banks, shares at savings and loan associations, demand deposits at commercial banks, and time deposits at commercial banks. It shall be assumed that the liabilities of all insurance companies and pension plans are exogenous variables. There are a number of reasons for this decision. First, the liabilities of these institutions change somewhat consistently from quarter to quarter, reflecting mainly the fulfillment of premium payments on long-term commitments (not strictly true of the liabilities of property and casualty insurance companies). Second, the volume of *new* funds flowing into these intermediaries is influenced greatly by nonmarket and noneconomic forces, such as population growth and attitudes toward risk and natural catastrophes. Finally, when a number of trial equations were estimated for these financial assets the results were that the only significant variable in the equation was the lagged stock of the particular asset.

The demands for the four remaining financial assets are treated as endogenous variables in the model. The additional notation used in these equations is as follows:

Y: Gross National Product

i_U: Interest rate on mutual savings bank deposits

i_S: Interest rate on savings and loan shares

i_{TD}:   Interest rate on commercial bank time deposits

The specification of these behavioral equations also follows the stock adjustment principle. The actual estimated regressions are

$$DD^c/Y = -.012\ i_{TB} - .019\ i_{TD} + .620\ (DD^c/Y)_{-1}$$
$$(3.91) \qquad (3.05) \qquad (5.74)$$
$$+ .046\ S_1 - .011\ S_2 + .031\ S_3 + .540$$
$$(7.53) \qquad (2.08) \qquad (5.39) \qquad (3.34) \qquad \textbf{(21)}$$
$$R^2 = .99 \qquad SE/DV = .014$$
$$SE = .013 \qquad DW = 1.71$$

$$TD^c/Y = .020\ i_{TD} - .008\ i_{TB} - .774\ (\Delta Y/Y_{-1})$$
$$(3.02)\qquad (2.72)\qquad (6.38)$$
$$+ .926\ (TD^c/Y)_{-1} - .027\ S_1$$
$$(18.5)\qquad\qquad (1.36)$$
$$- .004\ S_2 - .017\ S_3 + .046 \tag{22}$$
$$(.56)\qquad (1.50)\qquad (2.52)$$
$$R^2 = .99\qquad SE/DV = .018$$
$$SE = .011\qquad DW = 2.15$$

$$D^u/Y = .006\ i_U - .005\ i_{GB} + .787\ (D^u/Y)_{-1} + .044\ S_1$$
$$(2.71)\qquad (2.13)\qquad (10.7)\qquad\qquad (19.6)$$
$$+ .011\ S_2 + .022\ S_3 + .039$$
$$(6.53)\qquad (13.9)\qquad (2.15) \tag{23}$$
$$R^2 = .92\qquad\qquad SE/DV = .014$$
$$SE = .004\qquad\qquad DW = 1.77$$

$$D^s = .051\ Y - 382.2\ i_{GB} - 773.2\ i_{TD} + 1590.0\ i_S$$
$$(1.93)\qquad (1.54)\qquad (3.04)\qquad (4.16)$$
$$+ .976\ D^s_{-1} - 61.9\ S_1 + 190.3\ S_2$$
$$(40.0)\qquad\quad (.18)\qquad\quad (.81)$$
$$- 738.6\ S_3 - 5531.3 \tag{24}$$
$$(2.63)\qquad (2.42)$$
$$R^2 = .99\qquad\qquad SE/DV = .005$$
$$SE = 247.3\qquad\qquad DW = 1.89$$
$$RHO = .15$$

The desired level of each financial asset is a function of the own rate of interest, rates on alternative assets, and a constraint variable. In all of the equations just recorded, GNP is the constraint variable. Although some authors have used wealth as a portfolio constraint[3] the measurement problem indicated that the income variable might still be more appropriate. The ratio-versus-linear specification is also obvious in Equations 21 through 24. In all cases we tried both formulations and chose the regression that performed best (based on t-values, a priori signs of the coefficients, and rapid speeds of adjustment).

Equation 21 describes the demand for demand deposits. The Treasury bill rate and time deposit rate appear with negative coefficients, whereas the positive (and significant) constant term suggests that DD^c

---

[3] See [12] and [24]. Income has also been used by one of these authors (with regard to the time deposit equation), that is, De Leeuw and Gramlich [14], suggesting that wealth and income are interchangeable to some extent.

increases as Y increases (the implied coefficient of Y is derived by linearizing Equation 21; it consists of the constant term and the coefficients of i_{TB} and i_{TD} multiplied by their respective levels). The speed of adjustment in DD^c demand is rather quick, that is, 38 percent after one period and 85 percent after one year.

Equation 22 is the demand for commercial bank time deposits. The specification is quite similar to the corresponding equation of the FRB-MIT model.[4] The demand for TD^c is positively related to i_{TD} and negatively related to i_{TB}. The long-term Government bond rate was tried as an alternative to i_{TB}, but it was less significant. This probably reflects the recent growth in the importance of time certificates of deposit (CD) and the high degree of substitutability between CD and Treasury bills. The negative sign attached to $\Delta Y/Y_{-1}$ reflects the lag in the impact of an increase in Y on demand for time deposits. An increase in GNP does not increase TD^c demand initially; after one period the expected positive relationship is restored. Thus, the longer-run impact of an increase in Y is to increase TD^c demand. This can be demonstrated (as with DD^c demand) by linearizing Equation 22 and showing that the coefficient of Y is positive. The speed of adjustment in TD^c demand is slow; only 7 percent is completed after one period, or 25 percent after one year.

The demand for mutual savings bank deposits is reported in Equation 23. The demand for D^u is positively related to the own rate, i_U, and negatively related to the Government bond rate. The Treasury bill rate was tried here instead of i_{GB}, but the latter had a much higher t-value. The impact of an increase in Y is to raise D^u, as one would expect (the results can be demonstrated, as before, by linearizing Equation 23). The speed of adjustment is rather quick; that is, over 21 percent is completed in the first period, and more than 60 percent is achieved after one year.

The demand for savings and loan shares (Equation 24) is the only one of the four demand equations that is in linear rather than ratio form. The ratio specification had an infinite speed of adjustment (as was found with some of the security demand equations of Chapter 3). The demand for D^s is positively related to the own rate of interest and negatively related to i_{GB} and i_{TD}. The level of GNP also appears with a positive coefficient, as was expected. The speed of adjustment is very slow; that is, only 2.4 percent of adjustment occurs in the first period, or slightly less than 10 percent is completed after one year.

The overall performance of the demand equations for the liabilities of financial intermediaries is encouraging. The low standard errors and

[4] See [14].

the absence of serial correlation (except in Equation 24 where the auto-regressive structure had to be estimated) indicate that the estimated equations are statistically sound. The rather rapid speeds of adjustment found for DD^c and D^u lends economic credibility to the behavioral equations. The equations also support the contention that the liabilities of financial intermediaries are substitutes for each other (to some extent) and for open market securities in the public's portfolio.

SUPPLY OF FINANCIAL ASSETS

In the previous section, demand equations for four endogenously determined financial assets were presented, namely, demand deposits, time deposits, mutual savings bank deposits, and savings and loan shares. These assets are "supplied" by financial institutions and, therefore, ought to have either simple supply equations or interest-rate-offered equations so that the volume of, and the rate on, each asset can be determined endogenously. As we mentioned earlier, there is a legal prescription for the rate on demand deposits, that is, zero, so that such a rate will not appear in the model. As the first of our three equations to be eliminated from the final model (corresponding to the three rates legally fixed at zero), a supply equation for demand deposits is not specified.

Since the other three liabilities of financial intermediaries were viewed as constraints by the institutions we ought to specify interest-rate-offered equations for each financial asset. There is, however, a severe data problem in these cases that forces us to abandon this approach. The yields on time deposits, savings deposits, and savings shares are available only annually, whereas our model is based on quarterly observations, implying a quarterly decision-making process. The FRB-MIT model has skirted this issue by estimating an annual equation for the time-deposit-rate offered, after which a quarterly interpolation for the equation is derived. Although this procedure does not really make the rates generated endogenous from the behavioral point of view, we shall append a modified version of the FRB-MIT time-deposit-rate-offered equation[5] to our model in order to have the maximum time deposit rate included in the reduced-form equations of Chapter 5. The rates on savings and loan shares and mutual savings bank deposits will be considered exogenous variables. The only new variable that appears in the i_{TD} equation is i_{MTD} or the maximum time deposit rate permitted for commercial banks under Regulation Q. The quarterly interpolation of the annual equation (estimated using data

[5] See [27] for a discussion of this equation.

between 1955 and 1965) is

$$i_{TD} = -.362 + .0158 \, [L^c/(DD^c + TD^c)] + .016 \, i_{CB}$$
$$+ .463 \, i_{MTD} - .360 \, i_{MTD-1} + .869 \, i_{TD-1} \qquad (25)$$
$$R^2 = .975 \qquad DW = 2.55 \quad \text{(for annual eq.)}$$
$$SE = .028$$

The rate offered by commercial banks on time deposits is positively related to the percentage of the portfolio in commercial loans (because of the high rate of return on these assets), positively related to the corporate bond rate and positively related to the maximum time deposit rate.

MARKET FOR HIGH-POWERED MONEY

High-powered money consists of reserves at commercial banks and currency held by the public. The supply of high-powered money is determined (primarily) by open market operations of the "Fed" plus borrowings by commercial banks at the "Fed." Open market operations are to be considered the exogenous policy variable of the monetary authority. Changes in unborrowed reserves plus currency are (almost) in one-to-one correspondence with open market operations. The supply of unborrowed reserves plus currency, or Z, is exogenous. The total supply of high-powered money, Z plus borrowings by banks at the "Fed" (B^c), must be equal to total demand as an equilibrium condition. Total demand consists of the demands for currency, required reserves (at banks), and excess reserves (at banks). The market clearing condition can be expressed (after bringing all endogenous variables to the right-hand side) as follows:

$$Z = RR + ER^c - B^c + CUR \qquad (26)$$

where RR is required reserves and CUR is currency. Equations have already been specified for ER^c and B^c in Chapter 3. In order to complete the market for high-powered money, demand equations for required reserves and currency must be specified. These two equations use the following additional notation.

k_1:   Required reserves ratio on DD^c

k_2:   Required reserves ratio on TD^c

θ_1:   Proportion of public deposits that are demand deposits

θ_2:   Proportion of public deposits of that are time deposits

The two demand equations are

$$RR = k_1 DD^c + k_2 TD^c + (\theta_1 k_1)(\theta_2 k_2)(D + T)^c{}_G \qquad (27)$$

$$
\begin{aligned}
CUR = &-1916.0\ i_{GB} + .119\ Y + .283\ CUR_{-1} - 1125.6\ S_1 \\
&\quad (1.95) \qquad\quad (3.55) \qquad (1.74) \qquad\qquad\quad (1.33) \\
&-777.2\ S_2 - 371.1\ S_3 + 16659.0 \\
&\quad (1.22) \qquad (.54) \qquad\quad (2.06) \\
&R^2 = .78 \qquad\qquad\qquad SE/DV = .046 \\
&SE = 1539.8 \qquad\qquad DW = 2.13
\end{aligned}
\qquad (28)
$$

Equation 27 is a definition. Required reserves at banks is defined as equal to the required reserves ratio on DD^c times the volume of DD^c plus the required reserves ratio on TD^c multiplied by the volume of TD^c plus a weighted average of the two required reserves ratios multiplied by the total amount of public deposits. Equation 28 describes the demand for currency by the public. Currency demand is positively related to GNP and negatively related to the Government bond rate. The lagged dependent variable indicates a rather quick speed of adjustment; that is, over 70 percent of adjustment is completed after one quarter. It should be noted that i_{TB} was tried instead of i_{GB} because it has been argued frequently that the short-term rate is the relevant opportunity cost in determining optimal cash balances. The Treasury bill rate does, in fact, appear in the demand deposit equation. In Equation 28, however, i_{TB} was not nearly significant when it was tried. This was true both for linear and ratio specifications of the demand for currency.

There is no separate supply equation for currency. The "Fed" is assumed to determine the volume of unborrowed reserves plus currency as a single exogenous supply variable. The absence of a separate currency supply equation is the second of three potential equations that are missing from the model (a supply equation for DD^c was the first) corresponding to the three interest rates that are legally set equal to zero.

The fact that Equation 26 is an equilibrium condition for a financial asset (high-powered money) without an *explicit* interest rate to "determine" will be quite important for the discussion in the next section on interest rate determination. The interest rate on "Z" is legally set equal to zero. Equation 26 obviously does not "determine" Z as Equation 27 "determines" RR because Z is exogenous. Each of the four variables on the right-hand side of Equation 26 has an explicit equation, so that none of them are defined by it. The influence of the equilibrium condition expressed in Equation 26 will be examined in detail in the next section.

INTEREST-RATE DETERMINATION FOR SECURITIES

In a model that determines as endogenous variables the total supply, total demand, and the interest rate of a single particular security, the equilibrium condition setting quantity demanded equal to quantity supplied can be said to determine the interest rate. Our model differs from this simple prototype in at least three basic ways. First, as has been stressed above, there are three interest rates that are not free to vary. Second, the total demand for each security is not endogenous. Certain parts of Government bond demand, corporate bond demand, and so on are exogenous. Third, because this econometric model determines a large number of variables that form different markets within the model, it is incorrect from the theoretical point of view to identify one particular equation with the determination of one particular variable. In a general equilibrium framework all variables are simultaneously determined.

Despite the simultaneous determination of all variables in our model, we shall identify particular equations with the determination of certain variables. This is certainly important for expository purposes. It is also possible to identify the primary forces influencing a particular variable. In the following discussion, therefore, when it is said that Equation X determines variable Y, the qualification regarding the simultaneous determination of all variables is to be understood. The rates on corporate bonds, mortgages, and state-local bonds are, in fact, determined by the simple market-clearing mechanisms. The relevant equations are

$$CB^u + CB^l + CB^p + CB^x = \overline{CB} \qquad (29)$$

$$M^u + M^s + M^c + M^l + M^x = \overline{M} \qquad (30)$$

$$SL^c + SL^o + SL^x = \overline{SL} \qquad (31)$$

where CB^x is the exogenous portion of CB demand, M^x is the exogenous part of M demand, SL^x is the exogenous portion of SL demand, and SL is exogenous state-local bond supply.

The long-term Government bond rate, i_{GB}, could also be determined by setting the various demands for Governments equal to exogenous supply. The alternative, used in other models of the financial sector,[6] is to tie the long-term Government bond rate to the Treasury bill rate in a term structure formulation. We have also chosen to use the term structure relationship for a number of reasons. First, only 58 percent of Government bond demand is endogenous (using the data for the end of 1965). Corporate, household, and state-local government demands for U.S. Government securities are exogenous. If a significant portion of the demand for a security is exogenous, then the equilibrating mechanism imposed by a market-clearing equation can produce very unrealistic movements in the interest rate.[7] This is especially true if the most interest-sensitive demands are not included in the model. The real-world absorption of an increment in Governments may be very different from what would be implied by a simple market-clearing condition. The activities of security dealers in Governments has also been ignored here, whereas the impacts of the "Fed's" open market operations and Treasury financing certainly are buffered by the security dealers. The second reason for not using a market-clearing condition in favor of a term structure equation is that empirically there has been a rather stable relationship between the Treasury bill rate and the long-term Government bond rate. If it were possible to estimate individual demand equations for short-term and long-term Governments for each intermediary and the other important sectors in the market, then separate supply-equals-demand conditions in the two markets would be sufficient to explain the short-long relationship. This approach is not feasible. Trial attempts were made at estimating demands for "shorts" relative to "longs" for all of the institutions similar to the equation that was estimated for commercial banks. They were unsuccessful. Even if they had succeeded, however, the activities of security dealers and corporations, which are probably important in this area, would still have been missing.

The term structure equation that shall be used is taken from the work of Hamburger and Latta.[8] The estimated equation is

$$i_{GB} = .124 + .949 \ i_{GB-1} + .234 \ i_{TB} - .206 \ i_{TB-1}$$
$$\phantom{i_{GB} = .124 +} (23.5) \phantom{i_{GB-1} +} (7.67) \phantom{i_{TB} -} (7.00)$$
$$R^2 = .977$$
$$SE = .094 \qquad\qquad (32)$$
$$DW = 2.02$$

---

[6] See [12] and [22].

[7] This might be one reason for the lack of a supply-equals-demand equation in the Goldfeld model [22]. Although his model has only one Government bond demand as endogenous, the underlying reasoning is still the same in our case.

[8] See [25].

This equation was chosen because of its relatively simple specification together with rather good performance. The standard error is nine basis points, which compares favorably with other term structure equations that have been estimated.

The last rate on open market securities in the model is the Treasury bill rate. This rate can be thought of as being "determined" in the market for high-powered money[9] by Equation 26. Given the real sector of the economy, that is, GNP, the only variable that can equilibrate the demands for Z with the exogenous supply is i_{TB}.[10] The Treasury bill rate adjusts so that the demands for required reserves (via demands for DD^c and TD^c that are functions of i_{TB}), excess reserves, borrowings, and currency (via the effect of i_{TB} on i_{GB} and the latter's impact on currency demand) are brought into equality with the exogenous level of Z supplied by the "Fed."

The Treasury bill rate could have been determined by estimating demands for short-term Governments and setting them equal to exogenous supply. This was not done for the same reasons just cited in connection with the use of a term structure equation to determine i_{GB}. The absence of this equilibrium condition setting demand for "shorts" equal to supply is the third relationship missing from our model in connection with the three interest rates set equal to zero.

It does not seem to be unrealistic to view the Treasury bill rate as being determined in the money market, as has been done here. It means, simply, that the active decision can be recorded in the money market demand equations, the assumption being that the demands for bills are adjusted accordingly as a residual. Until a more comprehensive set of data is compiled with regard to the short-long breakup in Government bond holdings, the formulation set forth here is the only realistic choice.

REAL SECTOR OF THE MODEL

In the previous section it was pointed out that i_{TB} is determined in the market for high-powered money because, with GNP given, only the Treasury bill rate can equilibrate Equation 26 above. It now seems most appropriate to set forth the real-sector equations that "determine" GNP and its components. The new notation that will be used in the real-sector

---

[9] For a similar conclusion see [27], pp. 43–44.
[10] Although i_{GB} appears in the currency demand equation, it cannot act independently because of Equation 32.

equations is as follows:

II: Inventory investment

RC: Residential construction

C: Consumption

CU: Capacity utilization

MUO: Manufacturers unfilled orders

LA: Length of amortization on mortgages

PRC/P_c: Rent component of the consumer price index divided by the consumer price index

Y^p: Personal income

TX: Personal taxes

G: Government expenditure

α_1, α_2: Constants relating TX to Y^p

β_1, β_2: Constants relating Y^p to GNP

The demand components of GNP that will be treated as endogenous variables are consumption (total), corporate investment, inventory investment, and residential construction. The behavioral equations are all specified in real terms; that is, the dollar variables are divided by the GNP deflator, P. The eight equations that belong to the real sector are listed below, after which a brief discussion of each equation is presented.

$$
\begin{aligned}
I^c/P = \ &.013 \ Y/P + \ .133 \ \Delta L^c/P + \ 18.8 \ CU_{-1} \\
&(2.31) \qquad\quad (4.28) \qquad\qquad (3.14) \\
&+ .840 \ (I^c/P)_{-1} - 1479.4 \ S_1 \\
&\quad (14.6) \qquad\qquad\quad (13.08) \\
&+ 1540.0 \ S_2 - 213.5 \ S_3 - 190.72 \\
&\quad (14.7) \qquad\quad (2.03) \qquad\quad (2.74) \\
&R^2 = .98 \qquad\quad SE/DV = .027 \\
&SE = 221.0 \qquad DW = 1.73
\end{aligned}
\tag{33}
$$

$$
\begin{aligned}
II/P = \ &.146 \ \Delta L^c/P + \ 122.1 \ \Delta MUO_{-1} + \ .302 \ (II/P)_{-1} \\
&(1.64) \qquad\qquad (3.45) \qquad\qquad\quad (2.75) \\
&+ 1859.1 \ S_1 - 600.5 \ S_2 + 233.3 \ S_3 - 48.97 \\
&\quad (5.53) \qquad\quad (2.05) \qquad\quad (.87) \qquad\quad (.18) \\
&R^2 = .71 \qquad\qquad SE/DV = .917 \\
&SE = 612.0 \qquad\qquad DW = 2.18
\end{aligned}
\tag{34}
$$

$$RC/P = -294.5\ i_M + 92.8\ LA + .692\ \Delta HH + 38.8\ PRC/P_c$$
$$\quad\quad (1.77) \quad\quad (2.82) \quad\quad\quad (1.13) \quad\quad\quad (1.01)$$
$$+ .688\ (RC/P)_{-1} - 859.4\ S_1 + 1358.2\ S_2$$
$$\quad (7.70) \quad\quad\quad\quad (7.69) \quad\quad (6.99)$$
$$+ 909.7\ S_3 - 2927.7$$
$$\quad (8.25) \quad\quad (.64)$$

$$R^2 = .92 \quad\quad\quad\quad SE/DV = .044$$
$$SE = 252.3 \quad\quad\quad DW = 1.47$$

$$\tag{35}$$

$$C/P = .738\ Y^d/P + .223\ (C/P)_{-1} - 11536.0\ S_1$$
$$\quad\quad (5.19) \quad\quad\quad (1.42) \quad\quad\quad (8.70)$$
$$- 6634.7\ S_2 - 8528.3\ S_3 + 4846.0$$
$$\quad (15.1) \quad\quad (21.9) \quad\quad\quad (4.45)$$

$$R^2 = .99 \quad\quad\quad SE/DV = .011$$
$$SE = 888.4 \quad\quad DW = 1.91$$

$$\tag{36}$$

$$Y = C + I^c + II + RC + G \tag{37}$$

$$Y^p = \beta_1 + \beta_2 Y \tag{38}$$

$$TX = \alpha_1 + \alpha_2 Y^p \tag{39}$$

$$Y^d = Y^p - TX \tag{40}$$

The estimated demand equations for components of GNP, Equations 33 through 36, are rather standard specifications. Each equation can be derived from a flexible capital-stock adjustment mechanism. Each of the dependent variables can be thought of as a function of current and lagged values of the explanatory variables, where the Koyck distributed lag is assumed so that the lagged dependent variable incorporates the lagged values of the other explanatory variables.[11] Because the major concern of this study does not lie in the real sector, the final equations that were used were chosen for their simplicity as well as their statistical performance. How well this set of equations approximates the real world will become most clear in Chapter 5 when the impact multipliers are calculated.

Equation 33 describes corporate investment in plant and equipment. The positive coefficient attached to GNP probably reflects the positive relationship of internal funds to GNP and the positive impact of internal

---

[11] See [4] for a similar discussion.

funds on I^c. The L^c variable, commercial loans, was entered as a constraint to reflect credit rationing by banks. An increase in L^c presumably implies easier credit conditions and, hence, increased investment.[12] The capacity utilization variable has a positive coefficient, implying that investment increases as plant utilization approaches capacity. The absence of an interest rate variable from the investment function is unfortunate. All trial investigations using interest rates resulted in very low t-values for the coefficients of the rate variables, frequently with positive signs. It is possible that the specification of our investment function does not impose the *ceteris paribus* condition strongly enough.

Equation 34 is the inventory investment function. The commercial loan variable has a positive coefficient for reasons similar to those cited in connection with the corporate investment equation. The positive coefficient of manufacturers unfilled orders reflects the pressure of increasing backlogs on current inventory demand. GNP (minus II) was tried in Equation 34 as a proxy for the impact sales on inventory demand. Surprisingly, the variable was quite insignificant[13] and, therefore, was dropped from the final equation.

Equation 35 describes residential construction activity. The negative coefficient attached to i_M and the positive coefficient attached to the length of amortization (LA) suggest that terms of credit have an important influence on the housing market. This had been suggested by the presence of i_M in the mortgage supply equation (Equation 20) and is now corroborated here. The significance of LA implies that, in addition to interest cost, the length of time over which a mortgage can be repaid is important for RC activity. This is not supported by Equation 20, where LA does not appear to influence mortgage supply. Household formation has a positive impact on RC, as would be expected. The rent component of the consumer price index (relative to the consumer price index) also has a positive impact on RC. The latter is to be expected because higher rents make home building and ownership more attractive.

Equation 36 is the consumption function. It is quite simplified in a number of respects. First, durables and nondurables have not been separated, as has been done in other studies. Second, the only explanatory variable is disposable income. Wealth was tried, and so was liquid assets, but neither was significant. The speed of adjustment is quite rapid according to the very low coefficient attached to the lagged dependent variable.

---

[12] See [4].

[13] This is in direct conflict with the findings of Ando and Goldfeld [4]. The explanation lies probably in the superiority of their data compared with ours (which is Flow of Funds data). Note, however, that even their GNP variable is not strictly significant.

This is in agreement with the statements of Ando and Goldfeld regarding the reasonableness of a speeded-up consumption function.[14]

The four behavioral equations for GNP components are quite reasonable except for the inventory investment function. The speeds of adjustment are quick, there are no serial correlation problems, and the standard errors are quite low (except for Equation 34). The next group of equations in the real sector (Equations 37 through 40) are definitional equations and are not estimated.

Equation 37 defines GNP as the sum of consumption expenditure, corporate investment in plant and equipment, inventory investment, residential construction, and government expenditure. Actually the G variable includes not only government expenditure but also all the exogenous components of GNP, for example, exports minus imports and noncorporate business investment in plant and equipment.

Equation 38 defines personal income as linearly related to GNP. This is obviously an oversimplification.[15] The objective, however, is quite modest. In order to produce a meaningful set of multipliers in the next chapter, the endogenous nature of taxes should be taken into account. In order to do so, Y^p must be related to Y, taxes must be made a function of Y^p, and disposable income must be related to Y^p. Whether the simplified relationships recorded in Equations 38 through 40 are reasonable approximations to reality will become clear in Chapter 5. The value assumed for β_2 in Equation 38 is .77.[16] The value for β_2 is needed for the solution of the set of structural equations.

Equation 39 relates personal taxes to Y^p in a linear formulation. Once again this is oversimplified, but it turns out to be a reasonable approximation. The value of α_2 was set at .11 (see Footnote 16 for an explanation of how α_2 was calculated; it is the same as for β_2 with the appropriate changes). Equation 40 defines disposable income as equal to personal income less taxes.

COMMERCIAL LOAN MARKET

The commercial loan variable, L^c, has played an important role in the real sector of our model as outlined in the last section. This variable was also important in the bank portfolio equations recorded in Chapter 3.

---

[14] See [4].

[15] See the extended treatment given this relationship in the Ando-Goldfeld model [4].

[16] This is derived by taking ΔY^p for 1965 and dividing it by ΔY for 1965—a very crude approach but one that yields quite realistic multipliers in the next chapter.

The market for commercial loans is described by a demand equation (Equation 41, below) and an interest-rate-offered equation (Equation 42). The estimated regressions are

$$\Delta L^c = \underset{(6.00)}{.468} \ \Delta II - \underset{(1.10)}{450.0} \ \Delta i_{BL} + \underset{(6.75)}{.544} \ \Delta L^c_{-1}$$
$$R^2 = .78 \qquad SE = 406.0$$
$$DW = 1.98$$

$\qquad\qquad\qquad\qquad\qquad\qquad$ (41)

$$i_{BL} = \underset{(2.16)}{.275} \ i_M + \underset{(7.51)}{.191} \ i_{TB} + \underset{(5.46)}{.568} \ i_{BL-1} - \underset{(1.28)}{.059} \ S_1$$
$$+ \underset{(.32)}{.014} \ S_2 + \underset{(.32)}{.015} \ S_3 - \underset{(.42)}{.138}$$
$$R^2 = .96 \qquad\qquad SE/DV = .026$$
$$SE = .116 \qquad\qquad DW = 1.70$$

$\qquad\qquad\qquad\qquad\qquad\qquad$ (42)

The public's demand for commercial loans is recorded in Equation 41. This equation was taken from the FRB-MIT model[17] (after translating it into millions of dollars to conform with our unit of measurement). Commercial loan demand is positively related to inventory investment and negatively related to the bank loan rate. In connection with the impact multipliers of Chapter 5 we shall introduce another L^c demand equation of our own specification to contrast certain properties of the reduced form equations corresponding with each of these alternatives. Equation 41 as just recorded, however, will be considered the "basic" L^c demand regression.

The supply side of this market is represented by Equation 42, the interest rate offered by banks to potential loan customers. In Chapter 3 it was noted that we have assumed that commercial banks view ΔL^c as a constraint variable. The decision variable in this part of the banks portfolio, therefore, is the rate it charges, i_{BL}, and not the quantity supplied. This is the reason for the specification of supply as a rate-offered equation (the same was true for the time deposit market). Equation 42 implies that banks raise i_{BL} when other open market rates increase. In particular, the mortgage rate, i_M, and the Treasury bill rate, i_{TB}, are used as indicators according to our regression.[18]

---

[17] See [14].
[18] See [22], pp. 65–68, for further elaboration of the reasoning underlying the rate-offered formulation.

AN OUTLINE OF THE COMPLETE MODEL

The set of 42 equations presented in this chapter and in Chapter 3 determine the 42 endogenous variables of our model.[19] There are eleven markets within the structural model, as follows: the markets for (1) high-powered money, (2) Government bonds, (3) corporate bonds, (4) mortgages, (5) state-local bonds, (6) commercial loans at banks, (7) time deposits, (8) mutual savings bank deposits, (9) savings and loan shares, (10) demand deposits, and (11) the real sector, that is, GNP and its components. The equations that were presented in this chapter and Chapter 3 can be grouped according to the markets in which they belong in the following way. The market for high-powered money consists on the demand side of Equations 8, 25, and 35, whereas the supply side and market-clearing condition are expressed in Equations 9 and 36, respectively.[20] The market for Governments consists of demand Equations 1, 4, 10, 12, 15, and 17, whereas Equation 37 relates i_{GB} to i_{TB} in a term structure formulation. The corporate bond market consists of Equations 2, 13, and 18 on the demand side, Equation 19 on the supply side, and Equation 38 is the market-clearing condition. The mortgage market is made up of Equations 3, 5, 11, and 14 on the demand side, Equation 20 on the supply side, and Equation 39 is the market equilibrium condition. The market for state-local bonds is composed of Equations 6 and 16 on the demand side, and Equation 40 is the market-clearing equation (supply is exogenous). The commercial loan market consists of Equation 26 on the demand side and Equation 41 on the supply side. The time deposit market is made up of Equation 22 as the demand function and Equation 42 as the supply function. Neither of the last two markets requires a clearing equation because supply and demand refer to the identical aggregated variable. The markets for mutual savings bank deposits, savings and loan shares, and demand deposits are described by Equations 23, 24, and 21, respectively. The real sector of the model consists of Equations 27, 28, 29, and 30, representing the demands for components of GNP. Equations 31, 32, 33, and 34 determine GNP, personal income, personal taxes, and disposable income as endogenous variables.

These subsectors of the model that were just described do not function as individual systems. A disturbance in one market influences behav-

---

[19] A list of all of the endogenous variables, exogenous variables, and a condensed form of all of the structural equations appears in Appendix B.
[20] The equation numbers listed here refer to the numbering system used in the Appendix, which is different from that of the text.

ior in other markets through changes in GNP, portfolio constraints, and interest rates. In order to examine the interrelationship between the various markets, it is necessary to solve the system for the endogenous variables in terms of the exogenous variables; that is, the reduced form must be calculated.

This structural system of equations has also allowed us to draw conclusions regarding the substitute and complement relationships among securities. The security demand equations (presented in Chapter 3) from which we derived our results are, however, subject to the normal *ceteris paribus* conditions of demand theory. In other words, we have established whether an increase in the rate on security j will increase or decrease the demand for security i, before any other prices, rates, and other endogenous variables have changed. This is a valid concept of substitutes and complements in the simple Hicksian sense.[21] When we speak of butter and margarine as being substitutes for one another, it is this concept that we are implicitly using. On the other hand, there is another concept of substitutes and complements that deals with the demand relationships after all the other endogenous variables in the system (that is, all other prices, rates, and incomes) have equilibrated all markets except the two for which we are exploring the question of substitutability. This type of substitutability is the one that is relevant for the effects of monetary and fiscal policy. In other words, even though mortgages and Governments are complements, it does not necessarily imply that an increase in the money supply that will decrease the rate on Governments will decrease the demand for mortgages, implying a rise in the mortgage rate. The final "equilibrium" rate on mortgages will be influenced by what happens in all markets, especially, the corporate bond market, because mortgages and corporates are substitutes. In order to trace the influence of our basic substitute-complement relationships between securities through the entire market mechanism, we shall calculate the reduced form of our structural system of equations. This task, the assumptions involved, and the implications to be drawn will be explored in Chapter 5.

---

[21] Kuenne [35], pp. 124–129, discusses this concept of substitutes and contrasts it with the one mentioned toward the end of this paragraph.

Chapter 5

THE IMPACT MULTIPLIERS AND THEIR IMPLICATIONS

INTRODUCTION

The structural set of equations presented until now enabled us to examine the relationships among the various securities held by financial intermediaries. Given this information, it is now possible to go one step further and derive the implications of these substitute and complement relationships for monetary policy, fiscal policy, and capital market efficiency. Although we are able to conclude from the structural system how an individual institution will adjust its portfolio initially to an assumed change in market rates of interest and, therefore, how the intermediary reacts toward the risk relationship between securities, only the reduced form equations are able to trace the effects of monetary and fiscal policies through the market interrelationships to provide an answer to the question of the impacts of policy on financial and nonfinancial variables and vice versa. Before we specify the precise policy variables that are of interest and specify which financial and nonfinancial variables will reflect the impact of these variables, let us turn to a discussion of the nature and meaning of the reduced form equations.

A system of simultaneous equations can be represented as follows:

$$By + Gz = 0 \tag{i}$$

where B is the matrix of the coefficients of endogenous variables, y is the vector of endogenous variables, G is the matrix of the coefficients of predetermined variables, and z is the vector of predetermined variables. This system can be "solved" for the dependent (endogenous) variables in terms of the independent (predetermined) variables. This reduced form set of equations is represented in the following manner, with B^{-1} standing for the inverse of the B matrix:

$$y = -B^{-1}Gz = Pz \tag{ii}$$

where P equals $-B^{-1}G$. An element, p_{ij}, of the reduced form matrix, P, equals $\delta y_i / \delta z_j$, or the change in y_i induced by a unit change in z_j, with all other predetermined variables held constant. These impact multipliers produce the effect of a unit change in one predetermined variable, all others held constant, taking into account the market interrelationships between all endogenous variables.[1]

For a linear structural system the P matrix will be a constant matrix. The existence of nonlinearities complicates matters. Each nonlinear equation in the model must be linearized in order to produce a constant reduced form matrix.[2] This involves taking partial derivatives and evaluating them at a set of points (y_o, z_o). In our model, we have evaluated the relevant derivatives at the values of the fourth quarter of 1965. Because there are numerous lags in the model, these calculated impact multipliers, providing the impact of the predetermined variables on the endogenous variables during the current period, may vary considerably from the long-run response of an endogenous variable to a change in a predetermined variable.[3] The dynamic multipliers as well as the long-run equilibrium multipliers will, therefore, be calculated.

The impact multipliers of a change in any exogenous variable (which is not a lagged endogenous variable) over time can be calculated quite easily.[4] The P matrix in Equation ii can be partitioned into a matrix of

---

[1] This definition of impact multiplier is found in [20], p. 369.
[2] A complete discussion of the linearization procedure appears in Chapter III [21].
[3] See [22], Chapter V, pp. 69–70. It should be noted that we have linearized the system at the fourth quarter values for 1965 because the impact multipliers are strictly valid only in the neighborhood of the linearization and the latest values of the variables seemed to be the most reasonable choice.
[4] See [20], pp. 373–374.

the impact multipliers of lagged endogenous variables, P^a, and one of exogenous-variable multipliers, called P^b. Similarly, we can divide the z vector of predetermined variables into a vector of lagged endogenous variables, y_{t-1}, and a vector of all other exogenous variables, x. With this notation we can rewrite Equation ii as follows:

$$y_t = P^a y_{t-1} + P^b x_t \qquad\qquad \text{(iii)}$$

where the subscript t refers to the present time period, $t - 1$ refers to last period's values, and so on. We can lag Equation iii one period and substitute the expression for y_{t-1} back into Equation iii. This produces

$$y_t = P^b x_t + P^a P^b x_{t-1} + P^a P^a y_{t-2} \qquad\qquad \text{(iv)}$$

The impact multipliers of a once-and-for-all change in some exogenous variable in the x vector in period $t - 1$ on the endogenous variables of period t are derived by multiplying the P^a and P^b matrices. In order to derive the impacts of a once-and-for-all change in the policy variables on the endogenous variables of next period, the policy submatrix must be multiplied by the matrix containing the impact multipliers of lagged endogenous variables. Repeated application of this procedure produces the effects of the change in policy in period one on the endogenous variables of periods two, three, four, and so on.[5]

The interpretation of the various multipliers over time also requires some clarification. The reduced form equations of a simple linear system are $y = Pz$ rather than $dy = Pdz$, which is what we really have after linearizing the system by differentiating the set of equations and evaluating them at a point. Because $y = Pz$ also implies $\Delta y = P\Delta z$, the interpretation of the impact multipliers in the first period is the same for linear and linearized (originally nonlinear) systems. In the second period our impact multipliers, referring to a linearized system of equations, must again be interpreted as referring to *changes* rather than interpreted as *levels*. To get the final effect of the change in an exogenous variable on the *level* of the endogenous variables the impact multipliers of each period must be cumulated.

The long-run equilibrium multipliers can also be calculated by setting $y_t = y_{t-1} = y$. Imposing this condition on Equation iii produces

---

[5] The multipliers are strictly valid only in the neighborhood of the linearization. Because we do not relinearize the P matrix each period, the dynamic multipliers recorded here will be subject to some qualification.

$$y = (I - P^a)^{-1} P^b x \qquad\qquad (\text{v})$$

where I is the unit matrix.[6]

The impact multipliers to be reported will be examined with particular interest in a number of questions such as those that follow. What is the effect of changes in the degree of substitutability between securities on the efficacy of monetary policy?[7] What is the dynamic path of adjustment in the endogenous variables in response to changes in some of the exogenous variables? Are the bond markets "thin" according to the estimated equations of the model? How large is the impact of monetary policy on the real sector? These and other issues will be explored after calculating the impact multipliers of the basic model and the multipliers of certain variations of the basic model.

IMPACT MULTIPLIERS OF THE POLICY VARIABLES

GENERAL DESCRIPTION

The impact multipliers over time of selected policy variables are recorded in Tables I, I.A, I.B, I.C, I.D and Table II. The policy variables that are listed at the top of each column are unborrowed reserves plus currency (Z), the required reserves ratio on demand deposits (k_1), the required reserves ratio on time deposits (k_2), the discount rate (i_D), the maximum time deposit rate (i_{MTD}), government expenditure (G), the FHLB-borrowing rate (i_{FHLB}), and the marginal tax rate on personal income (α_2). Each element in a column records the impact of a change in the exogenous variable listed at the top on the corresponding endogenous variable listed in the extreme left-hand column. The unit of measurement has been translated from millions of dollars to billions of dollars in order to facilitate comparison with sets of multipliers calculated for other econometric models. For example, in Table I, which records the impact multipliers

---

[6] An equivalent way of deriving long-run equilibrium multipliers is as follows. Rewrite the structural model expressed in Equation i of the text as

$$Ay + By_{t-1} + Gz = 0$$

Setting $y = y_{t-1}$ produces $\quad (A + B)y + Gz = 0$

Solving for y products $\quad y = -(A + B)^{-1} Gz$

This last expression is the method used here to derive the equilibrium multipliers. Note, however, that the linearizations of the nonlinear equations are different in equilibrium (for example, after setting $A^o{}_t = A^o{}_{t-1}$) compared with the linearized equations used in the calculation of the simple reduced form. The qualifications regarding the validity of the dynamic multipliers just cited are even more significant for the equilibrium multipliers.

[7] This issue has been explored in [50].

for the initial quarter, the first entry in column one implies that a 1 billion dollar increase in Z causes GB^u to rise by .053 billion dollars (or 53 million dollars). The first entry in column two of Table I implies that a one percentage point increase in k_1 (for example, from .15 to .16) reduces GB^u by .132 billion. Finally, the first entry in column four suggests that a one percentage point increase in i_D (for example, from 2 percent to 3 percent) causes GB^u to fall by .01 billion dollars. Tables I, I.A, I.B and I.C record the multipliers for the first quarter, second quarter, third quarter, and fourth quarter, respectively. In order to get the final effect after one year, the individual multipliers in the first four quarters must be summed. This summation is done for five of the policy variables, and the results are recorded in Table I.D. The long-run equilibrium multipliers are reported in Table II. The calculation of the long-run multipliers was described at the end of the previous section.

Before discussing particular questions in light of the reduced form equations, it is important to examine the signs and magnitudes of some of the impact multipliers to ascertain the validity of the model as a whole. The effect of an increase in Z, for example, on market interest rates should be negative, just as increases in k_1 and k_2 should have positive impacts on rates. These signs are corroborated in the last seven rows of columns one through three of Table I. Tucker has suggested that, a priori, one would expect there to be an initial overadjustment in interest rates in response to a monetary action.[8] This has been found in other models of the financial sector.[9] The dynamic multipliers recorded in Tables I.A, I.B and I.C also show this "whiplash" effect on some interest rates (i_{TB}, i_{GB}, and i_{CB}). The effects of changes in Z, k_1, and k_2 on these interest rates after one year (recorded in Table I.D) are less than the initial impacts (presented in Table I on page 82). The long-run equilibrium impacts (which are shown in Table II) are also less than the initial impacts. More shall be said on the "dynamics" of the impact multipliers in later sections.

The magnitude of the government expenditure multiplier is also subject to certain a priori expectations. According to Table I the initial impact of an increase in G on Y is slightly larger than 2. The long-run impact in Table II is a little greater than 4. These figures are of the same order of magnitude found in other models of the U.S. economy.[10]

---

[8] See [51]. The lag in the demand deposit function causes this "whiplash" effect. Note, however, that only the rate that equilibrates this market (i_{TB}) must behave this way. The dynamics of other rates are determined by the lag patterns in the security demand equations (see discussion later).

[9] See [14] and [4].

[10] See [4].

Table I
Impact Multipliers of Selected Policy Variables: First Quarter

	Z	k_1	k_2	i_D	i_{MTD}	G	i_{FHLB}	α_2
GB^u	.053	−.132	−.120	−.010	.012	.097	−.002	−.097
CB^u	−.013	.033	.030	.003	−.002	.006	−.002	−.006
M^u	.198	−.494	−.450	−.038	.054	.094	.005	−.096
GB^c	.975	−2.434	−2.214	−.188	−.725	.456	−.002	−.458
M^c	.085	−.213	−.193	−.016	.080	−.013	−.001	−.013
SL^c	.080	−.200	−.182	−.015	.146	−.026	.000	−.026
GBS^c/GB^c	−.044	.109	.099	.008	.028	.017	.000	.000
ER^c	.082	−.039	−.035	−.003	.004	−.028	.000	−.029
B^c	.342	−.157	−.143	−.114	.015	.061	−.001	−.062
GB^s	−.104	.259	.236	.020	−.039	.077	−.080	−.077
M^s	.028	−.071	−.065	−.005	−.129	.023	−.114	−.022
GB^l	−.011	.028	.025	.002	−.003	.008	.000	−.008
CB^l	−.019	.048	.044	.004	−.018	.065	.018	−.063
M^l	.022	−.056	−.051	−.004	.007	−.019	.001	.019
GB^o	.181	−.453	−.412	−.035	.320	−.062	.001	.062
SL^o	−.080	.200	.182	.015	−.146	.026	.000	−.026
GB^p	.011	−.028	−.025	−.002	.002	.004	−.001	.005
CB^p	.037	−.093	−.084	−.007	.020	−.063	.015	−.062
$\overline{CB}$	.005	−.012	−.011	−.001	.001	.008	.000	−.008
$\overline{M}$	.334	−.834	−.759	−.065	.011	.085	−.108	−.087
DD^c	1.680	−4.202	−3.822	−.325	−1.127	.660	−.011	−.663

Table I (continued)

	Z	k_1	k_2	i_D	i_{MTD}	G	i_{FHLB}	α_2
TD^c	1.040	-2.603	-2.368	-.201	1.901	-.341	.006	.343
D^u	.169	-.422	-.384	-.032	.041	.190	-.003	-.190
D^s	.075	-.187	-.170	-.014	-.340	.059	-.001	-.060
CUR	.340	-.848	-.772	-.066	.087	.021	.000	-.021
L^c	.087	-.216	-.197	-.017	.018	-.044	-.005	.045
I^c	.013	-.034	-.031	-.003	.003	.021	-.001	-.022
II	.013	-.032	-.029	-.002	.003	-.006	-.001	.007
RC	.048	-.120	-.109	-.009	.002	.010	-.015	-.009
C	.078	-.193	-.176	-.015	.007	1.073	-.018	-2.087
Y	.152	-.379	-.344	-.029	.014	2.099	-.036	-2.110
Y^p	.117	-.292	-.265	-.023	.011	1.616	-.028	-1.625
Y^d	.105	-.262	-.239	-.020	.010	1.454	-.024	-2.828
TX	.012	-.029	-.027	-.002	.001	.162	-.003	1.202
RR	.237	.730	.664	-.046	-.075	.069	-.001	-.069
i_{TB}	-.730	1.823	1.660	.141	-.193	.519	-.008	-.522
i_{GB}	-.168	.419	.381	.032	-.044	.119	-.002	-.120
i_{CB}	-.238	.593	.540	.046	-.059	.156	.003	-.157
i_M	-.146	.364	.331	.028	-.005	-.032	.047	.027
i_{SL}	.711	1.776	1.616	.137	-.970	.313	-.006	-.315
i_{BL}	-.179	.448	.408	.035	-.038	.091	.011	-.092
i_{TD}	-.004	.010	.009	.001	.462	.002	.000	-.003

83

Table I.A
Impact Multipliers of Selected Policy Variables: Second Quarter

	Z	k_1	k_2	i_D	i_{MTD}	G	i_{FHLB}	α_2
GB^u	.017	−.010	−.009	−.009	.003	.083	−.003	−.105
CB^u	−.005	.005	.004	.002	.000	.004	.002	−.006
M^u	.103	−.141	−.128	−.040	.020	.113	.002	−.136
GB^c	.225	.008	.008	−.144	−.350	.030	.000	−.133
M^c	.105	−.215	−.196	−.029	.048	−.004	.000	.007
SL^c	.102	−.209	−.190	−.028	.082	−.007	.000	.013
GBS^c/GB^c	−.040	.074	.067	.012	−.021	.013	.000	−.016
ER^c	−.016	−.031	−.028	−.005	.003	.018	.001	.024
B^c	.024	.208	.190	−.072	.000	.071	−.002	−.085
GB^s	.003	−.067	−.061	.010	−.007	.033	−.036	−.050
M^s	.038	.078	.071	−.010	.072	.048	−.074	−.053
GB^l	−.004	.004	.004	.002	−.002	.006	.000	−.008
CB^l	.013	−.043	−.040	.000	−.007	.067	.014	−.081
M^l	.008	−.008	−.007	−.004	.002	−.016	.001	−.020
GB^o	.213	−.429	−.390	−.060	.174	−.016	.001	−.030
SL^o	−.102	.209	.190	.028	−.072	.007	.000	−.013
GB^p	.004	−.004	−.004	−.002	.001	−.002	−.001	.003
CB^p	.000	.020	.018	−.004	.008	−.054	.011	.067
$\overline{CB}$	.008	−.018	−.017	−.002	.001	.017	−.001	−.019
$\overline{M}$	.256	−.442	−.402	−.084	−.001	.142	−.072	−.162
DD^c	.423	−.074	−.067	−.256	−.387	−.020	−.006	−.128

Table I.A (continued)

	Z	k_1	k_2	i_D	i_{MTD}	G	i_{FHLB}	α_2
TD^c	.580	-.838	-.762	-.220	.763	.155	.001	-.079
D^u	.084	-.113	-.103	-.034	.015	.189	-.005	-.232
D^s	.053	-.087	-.079	-.018	-.140	.088	-.002	-.102
CUR	-.030	.275	.250	-.020	.020	.086	-.002	-.092
L^c	.065	-.111	-.101	-.021	.008	-.042	-.005	.052
I^c	.011	-.017	-.016	-.003	.001	.026	-.001	-.031
II	.000	-.006	.005	-.001	.001	-.002	.000	.003
RC	.031	-.048	-.043	-.011	.003	.017	-.008	-.018
C	.078	-.151	-.137	-.023	-.003	.535	-.019	-1.005
Y	.120	-.210	-.191	-.039	.004	.577	-.028	-1.051
Y^p	.092	-.161	-.147	-.030	.003	.444	-.022	-.809
Y^d	.083	-.145	-.132	-.027	.002	.400	-.020	-.728
TX	.009	-.016	-.015	-.003	.000	.044	-.002	-.081
RR	.070	-.036	-.033	-.038	-.022	.003	-.001	-.018
i_{TB}	.320	-1.225	-1.115	.014	-.031	-.027	-.004	-.089
i_{GB}	.070	-.282	-.256	.003	-.008	-.006	.000	-.021
i_{CB}	.100	-.390	-.355	.005	-.010	-.013	-.001	-.022
i_M	.008	-.106	-.097	.013	-.002	-.030	-.008	.037
i_{SL}	-.050	-.275	-.251	.085	-.324	-.125	-.001	.055
i_{BL}	-.040	-.009	-.008	.026	-.012	.038	.004	.059
i_{TD}	-.001	.002	.002	.001	.096	.002	.000	-.003

Table I.B
Impact Multipliers of Selected Policy Variables: Third Quarter

	Z	k_1	k_2	i_D	i_{MTD}	G	i_{FHLB}	α_2
GB^u	.009	.000	.000	−.007	.002	.068	−.003	−.092
CB^u	−.004	.004	.004	.002	.000	.003	−.001	−.005
M^u	.090	−.120	−.109	−.040	.024	.119	−.001	−.151
GB^c	.144	.044	.040	−.108	−.300	.008	.001	−.021
M^c	.123	−.216	−.196	−.039	.086	.010	.000	−.009
SL^c	.116	−.207	−.189	−.038	.138	.015	.000	−.012
GBS^c/GB^c	−.042	.068	.062	.015	−.028	.009	.000	−.012
ER^c	.010	.000	.000	−.004	.002	−.009	.000	.014
B^c	−.030	.079	.072	−.049	−.004	.044	−.002	−.063
GB^s	.007	−.043	−.039	.005	−.016	.022	−.016	−.034
M^s	.046	−.083	−.076	−.014	−.120	.069	−.048	−.081
GB^l	−.003	.002	.002	.002	−.001	.005	.000	−.007
CB^l	.024	−.057	−.052	−.005	−.010	.075	−.011	−.092
M^l	.006	−.004	−.003	−.003	.003	−.016	−.001	−.020
GB^o	.232	−.397	−.361	.077	.285	.033	.000	−.027
SL^o	−.116	.207	.189	.038	.138	−.015	.000	−.012
GB^p	.004	−.003	.003	−.002	.001	−.001	−.001	−.001
CB^p	−.008	.032	.029	−.001	.010	−.052	−.008	−.066
$\overline{CB}$	.011	−.021	−.019	−.003	.001	.027	−.001	−.031
$\overline{M}$	.267	−.423	−.385	−.097	−.006	.182	−.049	−.220
DD^c	.254	.081	.074	.191	.458	−.061	−.002	.033

Table I.B (continued)

	Z	k_1	k_2	i_D	i_{MTD}	G	i_{FHLB}	α_2
TD^c	.550	−.743	−.676	−.227	−1.029	.262	−.004	−.281
D^u	.075	−.092	−.083	−.033	.017	.181	−.005	−.233
D^s	.055	−.087	−.079	−.020	−.194	.100	−.003	−.123
CUR	.007	.094	−.085	−.015	.016	.052	−.002	−.072
L^c	.045	−.050	−.045	−.020	.009	.031	−.003	−.044
I^c	.007	−.008	−.008	−.003	.001	.028	−.001	−.035
II	−.003	.011	.010	.000	.001	.001	.000	.000
RC	.029	−.041	−.038	−.012	−.001	.021	−.004	−.025
C	.072	−.110	−.100	−.026	.002	.297	−.014	−.523
Y	.104	−.149	−.136	−.041	.002	.347	−.019	−.583
Y^p	.080	−.115	−.104	−.032	.002	.267	−.014	−.449
Y^d	.073	−.103	−.094	−.029	.001	.241	−.013	−.404
TX	.008	.011	−.010	−.003	.000	.027	−.004	−.045
RR	.048	.014	−.013	−.030	−.023	.001	.000	−.005
i_{TB}	.024	−.076	−.069	.005	−.022	.032	−.002	−.052
i_{aB}	.005	−.018	−.016	.001	−.005	.007	−.001	−.012
i_{cB}	.005	−.020	−.018	.003	−.005	.006	−.001	−.011
i_M	.025	.026	.024	.012	.003	.028	−.005	−.036
i_{sL}	−.090	−.004	−.003	.065	−.370	.128	.002	.141
i_{BL}	−.624	.012	−.011	.019	−.010	.020	.000	−.034
i_{TD}	−.001	.001	.001	.001	.077	.002	.000	−.002

Table I.C
Impact Multipliers of Selected Policy Variables: Fourth Quarter

	Z	k_1	k_2	i_D	i_{MTD}	G	i_{FHLB}	α_2
GB^u	.004	.007	.006	−.005	.001	.052	−.002	−.073
CB^u	−.004	.004	.004	.002	.000	.003	.001	−.004
M^u	.087	−.108	−.098	−.040	.024	.119	−.002	−.153
GB^e	.097	.038	.035	−.080	−.322	−.021	.000	.017
M^c	.135	−.216	−.197	−.045	.129	.025	.000	−.027
SL^c	.124	−.201	−.183	−.045	.195	.035	−.001	−.038
GBS^c/GB^c	−.042	.064	.058	.016	.040	.005	.000	−.007
ER^c	−.007	.006	.006	−.002	.003	−.005	.000	.008
B^c	.029	.032	.029	−.036	−.008	.028	−.001	−.043
GB^s	.007	−.029	−.026	.001	−.016	.017	−.007	−.025
M^s	.051	−.086	−.079	−.018	−.168	.084	.032	−.103
GB^l	−.002	.001	.001	.001	−.001	.005	.000	−.006
CB^l	.032	−.067	−.061	−.009	.011	.082	−.009	−.102
M^l	.004	−.002	−.001	−.003	.002	−.016	.000	.020
GB^o	.232	−.359	−.326	−.087	.390	.074	−.001	−.080
SL^o	−.124	.201	.183	.045	−.194	.035	.001	.038
GB^p	−.004	−.003	−.003	−.002	.000	.000	−.001	.000
CB^p	−.016	.040	.037	.003	.011	−.048	−.006	.063
$\overline{CB}$	.013	−.022	−.020	−.004	.001	.037	−.002	−.044
$\overline{M}$	.314	−.412	−.375	−.107	−.010	.212	−.034	−.262
DD^c	.154	.116	.106	−.138	−.487	−.061	.001	.069

Table I.C (continued)

	Z	k_1	k_2	i_D	i_{MTD}	G	i_{FHLB}	α_2
TD^c	.524	−.680	−.619	−.227	1.233	.312	−.007	−.376
D^u	.068	−.078	−.071	−.032	.015	.166	−.005	−.219
D^s	.058	.088	−.080	−.023	−.240	.106	−.003	−.134
CUR	.001	.033	.030	−.009	.010	.031	−.001	−.047
L^c	.030	−.020	−.018	−.017	.008	−.020	−.001	.031
I^c	.005	−.005	−.004	−.003	.001	.028	−.001	−.036
II	−.003	.008	.007	.000	.000	.002	.000	−.002
RC	.028	−.038	−.035	−.012	−.001	.023	−.002	−.028
C	.055	−.087	−.079	−.027	.000	.192	−.009	−.309
Y	.095	−.122	−.111	−.041	.000	.245	−.012	−.375
Y^p	.073	−.094	−.085	−.032	.000	.189	−.009	−.289
Y^d	.065	−.084	−.077	−.029	.000	.170	−.008	−.260
TX	.007	−.009	−.009	−.003	.000	.019	−.001	−.029
RR	.035	−.008	−.007	−.024	−.019	.003	.000	−.004
i_{TB}	.020	−.048	−.044	.000	−.013	.030	−.001	−.041
i_{GB}	.005	−.011	−.010	.000	−.003	.007	.000	−.010
i_{CB}	.003	−.010	−.009	.001	−.003	.006	.000	−.008
i_M	−.025	.028	.026	.012	.003	−.027	−.003	.034
i_{SL}	−.058	−.024	−.022	.048	−.372	−.117	.003	.149
i_{BL}	−.016	−.008	−.008	.014	−.007	.010	−.001	−.017
i_{TD}	−.001	.001	.001	.001	.067	.002	.000	−.002

89

Table I.D
One-Year Impact Multipliers of Selected Policy Variables

	Z	k_1	k_2	i_D	i_{MTD}	G
GB^u	.083	−.135	−.123	−.030	.015	.299
CB^u	−.026	.046	.041	.009	.002	.016
M^u	.483	−.864	−.786	−.159	.175	.446
GB^c	1.441	−2.343	−2.132	−.521	−2.157	.456
M^c	.443	−.860	−.782	−.132	.729	.018
SL^c	.422	−.818	−.744	−.126	1.126	.017
GBS^c/GB^c	−.168	.316	.287	.052	−.224	.042
ER^c	.048	−.063	−.058	−.014	.016	−.060
B^c	−.256	.162	.147	−.271	−.032	.205
GB^s	−.088	.121	.110	.036	−.108	.150
M^s	.163	−.319	−.290	−.048	−.973	.223
GB^l	−.020	.035	.032	.007	−.008	.024
CB^l	.050	−.119	−.108	−.010	−.067	.289
M^l	.041	−.069	−.063	−.014	−.019	−.066
GB^o	.856	−1.638	−1.490	−.259	2.279	.030
SL^o	−.422	.818	.744	.126	−1.127	−.017
GB^p	.022	−.038	−.034	−.007	.002	−.007
CB^p	.013	−.001	−.001	−.009	.072	−.217
$\overline{CB}$	.037	−.074	−.067	−.011	.007	.089
$\overline{M}$	1.130	−2.112	−1.921	−.353	−.050	.621
DD^c	2.515	−4.079	−3.710	−.910	−3.284	.518
TD^c	2.695	−4.864	−4.425	−.875	7.757	.387
D^u	.397	−.705	−.641	−.131	.110	.725
D^s	.241	−.448	−.408	−.075	−1.490	.353
CUR	.303	−.446	−.406	−.119	.101	.190
L^c	.227	−.397	−.361	−.076	.055	−.137
I^c	.036	−.064	−.058	−.012	.006	.103
II	.008	−.007	−.007	−.004	.002	−.005
RC	.135	−.247	−.225	−.043	−.007	.071
C	.292	−.541	−.492	−.092	.006	2.098
Y	.471	−.859	−.782	−.151	.007	3.267
Y^p	.362	−.662	−.602	−.116	.005	2.516
Y^d	.326	−.595	−.542	−.104	.005	2.264
TX	.036	−.066	−.060	−.012	.001	.252
RR	.391	.672	.611	−.138	−.149	.075
i_{TB}	−.366	.473	.430	.160	−.157	.554
i_{GB}	−.084	.109	.099	.036	−.036	.127
i_{CB}	−.129	.174	.158	.055	−.042	.154
i_M	−.186	.312	.283	.066	.013	−.116
i_{SL}	−.916	1.474	1.340	.335	−2.579	−.056
i_{BL}	−.259	.419	.381	.094	−.062	.158
i_{TD}	−.008	.014	.013	.003	.571	.008

As part of the general description of the impact multipliers, we shall break up the endogenous variables into three groups: interest rates, the real sector, and financial intermediary portfolios. In the next three sections we shall discuss the general pattern of the effects of the policy variables on each group of variables.

POLICY MULTIPLIERS ON INTEREST RATES: GENERAL DESCRIPTION

There are five instruments of monetary policy in our model: Z, k_1, k_2, i_D, and i_{MTD}. An increase in Z lowers interest rates, whereas an increase in k_1, k_2, or i_D raises interest rates. The explanation for these effects lies in the impact of these variables on the reserves market[11] (where i_{TB} is determined) and the subsequent effects on private rates via the term structure relationship and market substitutability. For example, an increase in Z implies that demands for RR, ER^c, and CUR must rise in order to satisfy the equilibrium condition expressed in Equation 26 of Chapter 4. A reduction in i_{TB} succeeds in satisfying that equilibrium. Similarly, an increase in k_1 causes RR to increase; hence i_{TB} must rise to reduce demand for (say) CUR. Finally, an increase in i_D lowers B^c; hence i_{TB} must rise to lower RR, CUR, and ER^c to maintain equilibrium.

The expected effect of changes in i_{MTD} on open market rates is not unambiguously clear, even from a theoretical standpoint.[12] There is good reason to believe that an increase in the maximum time deposit rate should raise the time deposit rate at banks but lower open market rates. Although the model set forth here leaves out certain aspects of a general theoretical model, the impact multipliers of i_{MTD} support the a priori expectation just presented.[13]

An increase in G and an increase in α_2 should raise and lower interest rates, respectively. The impacts occur through the effects of G and α_2 on Y and the necessary adjustments in i_{TB} to restore equilibrium to the "Z market." For example, because increases in GNP raise demands for DD^c and TD^c, interest rates must rise to maintain equilibrium in Equation 26 by reducing DD^c demand, TD^c demand, CUR demand, and ER^c demand.

The effect of changes in the FHLB rate should be felt most strongly on the mortgage rate. There is a direct reduction in mortgage demand by

---

[11] In simple models of GNP determination (for example, the IS-LM model), the effects of these policy variables on interest rates can be derived from the supply-equals-demand equation for money. The results are identical with the approach here.

[12] See [49].

[13] *Ibid.*, the dynamics of the response to i_{MTD} reported here are quite unrealistic and cannot be considered seriously. For this reason the evidence just presented must await additional results before a final judgment is made.

Table II
Equilibrium Multipliers of Selected Policy Variables

	Z	k_1	k_2	i_D	i_{MTD}	G	i_{FHLB}	α_2
GB^u	−.250	.331	.301	.112	−.036	−.254	−.003	.330
CB^u	.082	−.108	−.098	−.037	−.139	.693	−.003	−.897
M^u	−.588	.777	.707	.262	3.987	−2.286	.084	2.947
GB^c	2.207	−2.916	−2.652	−.984	−7.003	.454	−.020	−.584
M^c	2.300	−3.039	−2.765	−1.025	14.652	−.870	.040	1.120
SL^c	1.408	−1.860	−1.692	−.628	11.122	−.664	.031	.855
GBS^c/GB^c	−.038	.051	.046	.017	−.393	.312	−.009	−.403
ER^c	.008	−.011	−.010	−.004	.086	.069	.002	.089
B^c	−.034	.045	.041	−.431	−.351	.279	−.008	−.360
GB^s	.276	−.364	−.332	−.123	−2.178	.458	−.157	−.591
M^s	6.144	−8.118	−7.384	−2.739	−40.929	6.132	−.560	−7.908
GB^l	−.006	.008	.008	.003	−.065	.052	−.002	−.067
CB^l	3.258	−4.304	−3.916	−1.452	−10.114	3.518	−.200	−4.521
M^l	−.326	.431	.392	.146	1.123	−1.006	.023	1.299
GB^o	1.240	−1.638	−1.490	.552	9.813	−.648	.029	.835
SL^o	−1.408	1.860	1.692	.628	−11.122	.664	−.031	−.855
GB^p	−.022	.029	.026	.010	.057	−.283	.001	.367
CB^p	.299	−.395	−.359	−.133	.025	2.567	.003	−3.328
$\overline{CB}$	3.639	−4.808	−4.373	−1.622	−10.229	6.778	−.200	−8.748
$\overline{M}$	7.529	−9.948	−9.050	−3.357	−21.165	1.971	−.413	−2.541
DD^c	2.883	−3.808	−3.464	−1.285	−9.148	.593	−.027	−.763

Table II (continued)

	Z	k_1	k_2	i_D	i_{MTD}	G	i_{FHLB}	α_2
TD^c	5.139	−6.789	−6.176	−2.291	40.590	−2.425	.112	3.121
D^u	.544	−.719	−.654	−.242	−.574	.281	−.008	−.364
D^s	5.352	−7.071	−6.432	−2.385	−35.651	5.342	−.187	−6.888
CUR	.444	−.587	−.533	−.197	−.630	.354	−.010	−.456
L^c	.402	−.530	−.483	−.179	−.690	−.184	−.012	.240
I^c	.199	−.262	−.239	−.089	−.559	.370	−.011	−.478
II	.000	.000	.000	.000	.000	.000	.000	.000
RC	.618	−.816	−.743	−.275	−1.737	.151	−.034	−.189
C	1.573	−2.078	−1.890	−.701	−4.420	2.929	−.086	−5.077
Y	2.389	−3.156	−2.871	−1.065	−6.716	4.450	−.131	−5.743
Y^p	1.840	−2.430	−2.211	−.820	−5.172	3.427	−.101	−4.423
Y^d	1.656	−2.188	−1.990	−.738	−4.654	3.084	−.091	−5.345
TX	.184	−.243	−.221	−.082	−.517	.343	−.010	.923
RR	.513	.643	.585	−.228	.192	−.006	.000	.008
i_{TB}	−.077	.102	.093	.034	−.789	.627	−.018	−.809
i_{GB}	−.018	.023	.021	.008	−.181	.144	−.004	−.186
i_{CB}	.002	−.003	−.002	−.001	−.270	.463	−.006	−.599
i_M	−.586	.774	.704	.261	1.647	−.143	.032	.179
i_{SL}	−.330	.436	.397	.147	−2.658	.325	−.012	−.420
i_{BL}	−.407	.538	.489	.181	.700	.186	.012	−.244
i_{TD}	.000	.000	.000	.000	.753	.057	−.001	−.073

savings and loan associations when i_{FHLB} increases. Indeed, the impact multiplier of i_{FHLB} on i_M is positive, whereas the effects on other rates are almost negligible.

The longer-run impacts of policy on interest rates were discussed in the previous section in terms of the whiplash effects. As long as there are lagged relationships in the model, it is quite probable that this difference between short-run and long-run effects will persist. It is interesting to note that after one year the impacts of open market operations on i_M, i_{SL}, i_{BL}, and i_{TD} are greater than the initial impacts (compare Tables I and I.D). The whiplash effect suggested by Tucker is in evidence only for i_{TB}, i_{GB}, and i_{CB}. The lag in the DD^c equation that was used by Tucker to explain the existence of the overadjustment in rates (the lags in the B^c, ER^c, and CUR equations are also important) has its primary influence on i_{TB}, which equilibrates the market for high-powered money. The rates on Governments and corporates follow the dynamic pattern of i_{TB} because of the term structure relation and the high degree of substitutability between Governments and corporates. The dynamic paths of the other rates are more dependent upon the lagged relationships in their individual security demand equations and interest rate equations. Indeed, one of the defects of Tucker's explanation for whiplash effects in rates in response to monetary policy concerns his failure to recognize in his model more than one rate and, hence, an entire set of market-clearing equations.

After one year of adjustment the impacts on rates are of the same sign as the initial impacts. Note that the equilibrium response of each rate (see Table II) is also the same sign as the initial impact, except for i_{CB}. It is not, however, a requirement that long-run and short-run impacts be of the same sign. It is possible, for example, for GNP to rise by such a large amount after n periods so that an increase in (say) Z should reduce rates at first but raise rates in the long-run.[14] The initial and long-run effects of monetary policy on i_M are the same as for all other long-term open market rates. As was suggested at the end of the last chapter, the existence of the substitute relation between corporates and mortgages is most likely strong enough to make i_M react as other rates in response to exogenous shocks; that is, the corporate-mortgage relationship is "stronger" than the mortgage-Government relationship (complementarity does not dominate the behavior of i_M).

A major problem with the interest rate impact multipliers as recorded in Table I are the unstable results reported for i_{SL}. The initial impact of (say) a billion dollar increase in Z is to lower other long-term rates

[14] See [19].

(i_{GB}, i_{CB}, and i_M) by between 15 and 24 basis points (for example, from 2.00 to 1.85). The state-local bond rate, however, falls by 71 basis points according to Table I. A similar problem with i_{SL} is found for the other policy multipliers set forth in Table I. The problem lies in two characteristics of our model. First, there are only two endogenous demands for state-local bonds, one of which (for commercial banks) displays no interest sensitivity. This low degree of response to interest rates causes the rate to jump drastically when demand must be changed. Second, the market-clearing condition (which, in fact, forces changes in demand by other insurance companies when, say, TD^c falls, and SL^c demand is thereby reduced) imposes an unrealistic equilibrating burden on i_{SL}. It may be recalled that in Chapter 4 it was suggested that imposing an equilibrium condition on a market that has an insufficient level of its demand treated as endogenous can force the interest rate to behave peculiarly. Only 52 percent of SL demand is endogenous compared with 90 percent for mortgages and 90 percent for corporate bonds. Accordingly, two experiments were conducted with the basic model to test the hypothesis that these "unstable" results stemmed from the two reasons just cited. First, commercial bank demand for state-local bonds was made interest sensitive (and substitutes for Governments) by including an assumed coefficient of -500.0 attached to i_{SL} in GB^c demand, and an assumed coefficient of $+500.0$ was attached to i_{SL} in SL^c demand. The reduced form was then recalculated, and the results appear in Table III (for the first quarter). Second, a direct relationship was estimated linking i_{SL} to i_{CB}. The estimated equation is

$$i_{SL} = .736 \ i_{CB} - .460$$
$$(13.3) \qquad (1.80)$$

$R^2 = .80$ $\qquad SE/DV = .077$ $\qquad\qquad$ **(31a)**

$SE = .129$ $\qquad DW = 1.81$

$\qquad\qquad\quad RHO = .43$

This equation was then substituted for Equation 31, the market-clearing equation for state-local bonds. The reduced form was recalculated, and the results appear in Table III.A (for the first quarter). In both Tables III and III.A the only multipliers that appear are for interest rates and those others that were affected by the respective changes. In each case the impact multipliers for i_{SL} became of the same order of magnitude as for other long-term rates. In other words, increased substitutability *or* removing the equilibrium condition and replacing it with an "interest-rate equation" removes the unstable multipliers for i_{SL}. Because the structure of our model is based on a supply demand formulation, the basic

Table III
Selected Impact Multipliers with Increased Substitutability between Government and State-Local Bonds

	Z	k_1	k_2	i_D	i_{MTD}	G	i_{FHLB}	α_2
i_{TB}	$-.730$	1.823	1.658	$.141$	$-.192$	$.519$	$-.009$	$-.522$
i_{GB}	$-.168$	$.419$	$.381$	$.032$	$-.044$	$.119$	$-.002$	$-.120$
i_{CB}	$-.238$	$.594$	$.540$	$.046$	$-.059$	$.156$	$.003$	$-.157$
i_M	$-.146$	$.363$	$.331$	$.028$	$-.005$	$-.032$	$.047$	$.027$
i_{SL}	$-.172$	$.431$	$.392$	$.033$	$-.235$	$.076$	$-.001$	$-.076$
i_{BL}	$-.179$	$.448$	$.408$	$.034$	$-.038$	$.091$	$.011$	$-.092$
i_{rD}	$-.004$	$.010$	$.009$	$.001$	$.462$	$.002$	$.000$	$-.003$
GB^c	1.060	-2.649	-2.410	$-.204$	$-.607$	$.418$	$-.001$	$.420$
SL^c	$-.006$	$.015$	$.014$	$.001$	$.029$	$.012$	$.000$	$-.012$
GB^o	$-.006$	$.015$	$.014$	$.001$	$.064$	$.021$	$-.034$	$-.021$
SL^o	$.006$	$-.015$	$-.014$	$-.001$	$-.029$	$-.012$	$.000$	$.012$

Table III.A
Selected Impact Multipliers with a Direct Relationship between i_{SL} and i_{CB}

	Z	k_1	k_2	i_D	i_{MTD}	G	i_{FHLB}	α_2
i_{TB}	$-.073$	1.823	1.658	$.141$	$-.193$	$.519$	$-.009$	$-.522$
i_{GB}	$-.168$	$.419$	$.381$	$.032$	$-.044$	$.119$	$-.002$	$-.120$
i_{CB}	$-.238$	$.594$	$.540$	$.046$	$-.059$	$.156$	$.003$	$-.157$
i_M	$-.146$	$.363$	$.331$	$.028$	$-.005$	$-.032$	$.047$	$.027$
i_{SL}	$-.175$	$.437$	$.398$	$.034$	$-.043$	$.114$	$.002$	$-.116$
i_{BL}	$-.179$	$.448$	$.408$	$.035$	$-.038$	$.091$	$.011$	$-.092$
i_{TD}	$-.004$	$.001$	$.009$	$.001$	$.462$	$.002$	$.000$	$-.002$
GB^o	$-.005$	$.013$	$.012$	$.001$	$-.003$	$.007$	$-.002$	$-.007$
SL^o	$.006$	$-.014$	$-.013$	$-.001$	$.002$	$-.006$	$.001$	$.006$

model as set forth in Chapters 3 and 4 is still retained with the understanding that until state-local demand equations for other sectors are added, the multipliers on i_{SL} are unrealistic.[15]

POLICY MULTIPLIERS ON GNP: GENERAL DESCRIPTION

The impacts of monetary and fiscal policies on GNP are greater in the long run than initially. The multipliers cumulate over time. This is to be expected from the normal time dimension that is implicit in expenditure multiplier analysis. The effects of monetary policy on GNP are channeled through interest rate effects on RC and the impacts of commercial loans on I^c and II. Commercial loan demand is sensitive to the bank loan rate, so that I^c and II are indirectly related to i_{BL}.[16]

In our model, fiscal policy is much more effective than monetary policy, initially. In the long run, however, the impact on GNP due to, say, an open market purchase of one billion dollars is slightly more than one half the impact of a billion dollar increase in G. The effects of a percentage point change in k_1 or k_2 on GNP are greater than a billion dollar open market operation, although the oft repeated argument that reserve requirement changes are too blunt for countercyclical policy does not seem to be substantiated.

POLICY MULTIPLIERS ON PORTFOLIOS: GENERAL DESCRIPTION

The impacts of monetary and fiscal policy on the portfolios of financial intermediaries can be considered important side-effects of stabilization policy. An extensive treatment of this subject seems to be a worthwhile objective.[17] As a general approach one may use the following procedure. Take the multipliers of a model such as ours over the relevant time period for a stabilization goal, for example, one year. Adjust the magnitude of the multipliers so that each has the same impact on the stabilization objective, say, GNP. It is then possible to compare, for each financial intermediary's portfolio composition, the differential effects of using alternative stabilization tools to achieve a particular goal. Multiple goals can

---

[15] An attempt was made at estimating a household demand for state-local bonds, but the trial investigations were unsuccessful.

[16] We shall return to this question in a later section when comparing our monetary channel with those of other models.

[17] The author is currently engaged in research on this topic sponsored by the Federal Deposit Insurance Corporation.

also be analyzed, for example, a certain impact on GNP, given an interest rate constraint for a balance of payments objective.

One simplified example of the type of analysis just suggested is the following. From columns one and two of Table I it is possible to see that an open market purchase (*increase* in Z) of 2.5 billion has the same impact on income (Y) in the first quarter as a *reduction* of one percentage point in k_1. One can verify also that every element in column two is approximately 2.5 times the corresponding element in column one except for ER^c, B^c, and RR. For all other variables (and, hence, for portfolio items), open market operations and changes in reserve requirements on DD^c are equivalent. An increase in Z of 2.5 billion causes ER^c to increase by .20 billion, whereas a reduction of one percentage point in k_1 causes an increase in ER^c of only .04 billion. Recall that each of these policies has the same impact on GNP. On the other hand, an increase in Z of 2.5 billion causes RR to *rise* by .60 billion, whereas a decrease in k_1 of one percentage point causes RR to *fall* by .73 billion. Finally, B^c *falls* .85 billion when Z rises by 2.5 billion, whereas B^c *increases* by .16 billion when k_1 falls by one percentage point. The implications of these differential effects for such things as bank profits might enter as side-constraints in the execution of a given stabilization goal.

Experiments with the impact multipliers such as the example just given should provide new insight into the "side-impacts" of stabilization policies. Most other discussions of the side-effects of policy concentrate on the real sector. There is no reason, however, to ignore the financial sector in evaluating the advantages and disadvantages of alternative stabilization policies in terms of their side-effects in the economy.

PORTFOLIO SUBSTITUTABILITY AND MONETARY POLICY[18]

It was suggested in Chapter 1 that a low degree of substitutability between Government securities and private securities will decrease the efficacy of monetary policy. In particular, the lower the substitutability between securities, the smaller the impact of monetary policy on private rates of interest. If private investment were a function of these rates on private securities, then the impact on GNP will also be smaller with a reduced degree of substitutability. It should be noted that portfolio regulations on financial intermediaries tend to reduce substitutability between assets. For example, if an institution is limited in its holdings of some security to a certain percentage of its portfolio, then, when the limit becomes effective, the institution can no longer substitute in favor of that

[18] This section draws heavily on [50].

asset relative to others in response to an increase in yield. Regulations as to minimum holdings of a particular security have the same type of effects; for example, it is not possible to lower holdings below the minimum as yields fall. A rigorous demonstration, therefore, that reduced substitutability between securities reduces the efficacy of monetary policy would have important implications for the various regulatory agencies in charge of financial intermediaries.

Two experiments with the "basic" model were conducted in order to examine the "monetary policy substitutability hypothesis." First, the degree of substitutability between Governments and corporates was reduced to one half the original amount in the portfolios of mutual savings banks only. This was done by halving the coefficient of i_{GB} in Equation 1 and halving the coefficient of i_{GB} in Equation 2. The impact multipliers were then recalculated and the results appear for the interest rates, GNP, and its components in Table IV (for the first quarter). The reduction in the impact of monetary policy on the corporate bond rate is quite small. In Table I a unit increase in Z reduces i_{CB} by .238, whereas in Table IV the impact is minus .225. In other words, the difference is only one basis point. Similar results are obtained for changes in k_1 and k_2; that is, with the reduced substitutability the impact on i_{CB} is about 3 basis points less in both cases. The reduced impact on GNP is also of insignificant magnitude.

The second experiment reduces the degree of substitutability between all securities in all portfolios at the same time. The coefficients of all non-own rates of interest with negative signs (indicating substitutability) were reduced to one half their original size. The impact multipliers were then recalculated, and the results for interest rates, GNP, and its components appear in Table V (for the first quarter). Let us compare the impacts of a one billion dollar change in Z on private rates in Table V with the impacts recorded in Table I. The effect of a change in Z on i_{CB} is reduced by 13 basis points (more than one half) in Table V compared with Table I. The impact on i_M is also reduced by one half, whereas the impact on i_{SL} falls by 7 basis points or about 10 percent. The impact of Z on GNP is reduced by .05 billion, or almost one third. The latter comes almost entirely from the presence of i_M in the RC demand equation and therefore the lessened impact of a change in Z on RC. Had the corporate bond rate appeared in the I^c equation, the effect on GNP would have been reduced even more. Similar reductions in the efficacy of monetary policy due to reduced substitutability are to be found for the other policy variables in Table V compared with Table I.

The implications of the experiments conducted above for the possible effects of portfolio regulations on the efficacy of monetary policy are quite

Table IV
Selected Impact Multipliers with Reduced Substitutability for MSB

	Z	k_1	k_2	i_D	i_{MTD}	G	i_{FHLB}	α_2
i_{TB}	$-.731$	1.830	1.661	$.141$	$-.193$	$.520$	$-.009$	$-.522$
i_{GB}	$-.168$	$.420$	$.381$	$.032$	$-.044$	$.120$	$-.002$	$-.120$
i_{CB}	$-.225$	$.561$	$.511$	$.043$	$-.055$	$.146$	$-.003$	$-.148$
i_M	$-.140$	$.350$	$.318$	$.027$	$-.003$	$-.036$	$.047$	$.031$
i_{SL}	$-.712$	1.779	1.618	$.137$	$-.970$	$.314$	$-.006$	$-.315$
i_{BL}	$-.178$	$.445$	$.405$	$.034$	$-.037$	$.090$	$.011$	$-.091$
i_{TD}	$-.004$	$.009$	$.008$	$.001$	$.462$	$.002$	$.000$	$-.002$
I^c	$.013$	$-.033$	$-.030$	$-.003$	$.003$	$.002$	$-.001$	$-.021$
RC	$.046$	$-.115$	$-.104$	$-.009$	$.001$	$.012$	$-.016$	$-.010$
C	$.075$	$-.188$	$-.171$	$-.014$	$.006$	1.075	$-.018$	-2.088
Y	$.147$	$-.368$	$-.334$	$-.028$	$.013$	2.102	$-.036$	-2.113

Table V
Selected Impact Multipliers with Reduced Substitutability for All Portfolios

	Z	k_1	k_2	i_D	i_{MTD}	G	i_{FHLB}	α_2
i_{TB}	−.772	1.929	1.754	.149	−.204	.549	−.009	−.552
i_{GB}	−.178	.444	.403	.034	−.047	.126	−.002	−.127
i_{CB}	−.114	.285	.260	.022	−.028	.076	.001	−.076
i_M	−.077	.192	.175	.015	.012	−.076	.047	.072
i_{SL}	−.640	1.599	1.454	.123	−.951	.262	−.004	.264
i_{BL}	−.169	.421	.383	.032	−.036	.084	.011	−.086
i_{TD}	−.002	.005	.004	.000	.463	.001	.000	−.001
I^c	.012	−.030	−.028	−.002	.002	.022	−.001	−.022
RC	.025	−.063	−.058	−.005	−.004	.025	−.015	−.024
C	.052	−.129	−.117	.010	.000	1.090	−.018	−2.103
Y	.101	−.252	−.229	−.020	−.001	2.132	−.035	−2.143

clear. An increase in regulations will generally reduce the substitutability between securities in financial intermediary portfolios. The comparison of the impact multipliers in Table V with those of Table I imply that the efficacy of monetary policy, when measured by its effect on private rates of interest and (to some extent) GNP, is substantially lowered by a proliferation of portfolio regulations. The lesson to be drawn from the comparison between Tables IV and I is equally important. Imposing *one* regulation on *one* intermediary causing a reduction in *one* substitute relationship does not reduce the efficacy of monetary policy significantly. The fallacy of composition, however, once again appears in economic problems. Once regulations are imposed on all financial intermediaries, the reduction in the efficacy of monetary policy is quite substantial. A myopic approach to the effect of regulations on the efficacy of policy will give very misleading results. The individual regulatory agencies ought to be cognizant of the effects of their individual, but simultaneously enacted, portfolio regulations.

THE STRENGTH OF MONETARY POLICY: ANOTHER FORMULATION

The *initial* impacts of monetary policy on GNP recorded in Table I are quite small in comparison with the findings of Ando and Goldfeld.[19] For example, a one billion dollar increase in Z raises GNP by .152 billion in the first quarter according to our model, whereas Ando and Goldfeld find an impact of 1.91 billion for a billion dollar increase in Z.[20] The key difference between the two models seems to be the channel through which monetary policy operates. In our model it is interest rates (i_M and i_{BL}; the latter via the impact of i_{BL} on L^c and the effect of L^c on I^c), whereas the Ando-Goldfeld model has an additional (direct) impact of monetary policy on spending. That model uses a "potential-demand-deposit variable," DD^*, to reflect the direct impact of "credit availability" on commercial loans and the resulting impact on investment.

In order to see how the impact multipliers of monetary policy are changed in our model with the introduction of this "direct monetary channel," the following estimated equations were incorporated into our structure.

---

[19] See [4].
[20] Note that the FRB–MIT model also finds *small* initial impacts of monetary policy. See [14].

$$ER^c = -32.3 \; i_{TB} + .025 \; \Delta DD^* + .622 \; ER^c_{-1} + 93.3 \; S_1$$
$$ (1.59) \qquad (3.62) \qquad\qquad (4.32) \qquad\qquad (1.44)$$
$$+ \; 34.8 \; S_2 + 58.7 \; S_3 + 226.5$$
$$ (.94) \qquad (1.53) \qquad (1.53) \qquad\qquad\qquad \textbf{(10a)}$$
$$R^2 = .76 \qquad\qquad\qquad SE/DV = .112$$
$$SE = 60.9 \qquad\qquad\qquad DW = 2.32$$

$$B^c = 47.3 \; (i_{TB} - i_D) - .072 \; \Delta DD^* + .829 \; B^c_{-1} - 707.2 \; S_1$$
$$ (.50) \qquad\qquad\quad (5.26) \qquad\qquad (12.7) \qquad\qquad (4.80)$$
$$- \; 233.7 \; S_2 - 274.1 \; S_3 + 425.7$$
$$ (2.84) \qquad (3.33) \qquad (6.17) \qquad\qquad\qquad \textbf{(11b)}$$
$$R^2 = .86 \qquad\qquad\qquad SE/DV = .258$$
$$SE = 114.3 \qquad\qquad\qquad DW = 2.40$$

$$L^c = .660 \; II - 1995.8 \; (i_{BL} - i_{TB}) + .265 \; DD^* + .914 \; L^c_{-1}$$
$$ (1.77) \qquad (2.85) \qquad\qquad\qquad (2.99) \qquad\quad (24.6)$$
$$- \; 1752.0 \; S_1 + 1706.3 \; S_2 - 221.4 \; S_3 - 24680.0$$
$$ (1.58) \qquad\quad (2.32) \qquad\quad (.33) \qquad (2.77) \qquad\qquad \textbf{(41a)}$$
$$R^2 = .99 \qquad\qquad\qquad SE/DV = .022$$
$$SE = 1293.6 \qquad\qquad\qquad DW = 2.69$$

$$DD^* = (Z - CUR - k_2 TD)/k_1 \qquad\qquad \textbf{(43)}$$

The last equation (Equation 43) defines the new potential demand deposit variable, DD^*. The "revised" version of the model, therefore, contains an additional endogenous variable, DD^*, and an additional equation (Equation 43). Equation 41a replaces the old equation 41, that is, the demand for commercial loans by the public. The presence of the DD^* variable in Equation 41a with a positive sign reflects the direct (availability) impact of easier monetary policy, signified by an increase in DD^* (via increases in Z or reductions in k_1 or k_2), on commercial loans outstanding. It is the incorporation of this "availability variable" into the commercial loan market that makes monetary policy more effective, as shall be demonstrated. The first two equations just listed (10a and 11b) replace the original equations 10 and 11, the demands for excess reserves and borrowings, respectively. The only change is that ΔDD^* replaces ΔR^u, so that the effects of the new variable are integrated more completely into the model.

After adding Equations 10a, 11b, 41a, and 43 to the original structural equations, the impact multipliers are calculated. The results for monetary policy appear in Table VI (for the first quarter). The impact of monetary policy on income is now much larger than before. A unit increase in Z increases income by 1.21 billion compared with .15 billion recorded

Table VI
Impact Multipliers of Selected Monetary Policy Variables with a Direct Monetary Channel (First Quarter)

	Z	k_1	k_2	i_D	(k_1)
GB^u	.078	−.126	−.094	.006	−.082
CB^u	.003	−.072	−.003	.005	.008
M^u	.125	−.078	−.150	−.026	−.211
GB^c	−.974	4.308	1.171	−.568	−.156
M^c	.263	−.641	−.316	.047	−.208
SL^c	.028	.038	−.033	−.017	−.073
GBS^c/GB^c	−.082	.173	.098	−.009	.076
ER^c	.168	−.289	−.202	.006	−.190
B^c	−.480	.869	.576	−.072	.521
GB^s	−.013	−.118	.016	.028	.082
M^s	.027	−.036	−.033	−.001	−.035
GB^l	−.002	−.012	.002	.003	.009
CB^l	.069	−.224	−.083	.025	−.025
M^l	−.007	.050	.008	−.009	−.012
GB^o	.062	.090	−.075	−.038	−.165
SL^o	−.028	−.038	.034	.017	.073
GB^p	.000	.014	.000	−.003	−.008
CB^p	.024	.024	−.029	−.005	−.040
$\overline{CB}$	.096	−.272	−.115	.025	−.057
$\overline{M}$	.409	−.705	−.491	.012	−.467
DD^c	1.240	−1.099	−1.490	−.168	−1.897
TD^c	.366	.496	−.440	−.216	−.951
D^u	.191	−.304	−.229	.001	−.227
D^s	.071	−.096	−.085	−.003	−.093
CUR	.190	−.046	−.228	−.050	−.349
L^c	1.853	−5.283	−2.227	.488	−1.094
I^c	.262	−.745	−.315	.069	−.155
II	.271	−.771	−.325	.071	−.160
RC	.058	−.098	−.069	.001	−.066
C	.618	−1.691	−.742	.147	−.400
Y	1.209	−3.306	−1.452	.289	−.781
Y^p	.931	−2.546	−1.119	.223	.602
Y^d	.838	−2.291	−1.006	.201	−.541
TX	.093	−.254	−.111	.022	−.060
RR	.162	1.204	1.007	−.027	1.061
i_{TB}	−.105	−.789	.126	.193	.582
i_{GB}	−.024	−.181	.029	.044	.134
i_{CB}	−.027	.263	.033	.065	.186
i_M	−.176	.300	.211	−.004	.202
i_{SL}	−.206	−.465	.248	.160	.625
i_{BL}	−.068	−.068	.082	.036	.167
i_{TD}	.000	−.004	.001	.001	.003
DD^*	6.596	−12.588	−7.928	.477	−6.859

in Table I. The main difference can be traced to the larger impacts of the open market operation on I^c and II via the L^c variable (through the effect of Z on DD^*, and DD^* on commercial loans). In Table I, column one, the impacts on I^c, II, and RC are .013, .013, and .048, respectively; whereas in Table VI the impacts on I^c, II, and RC are .262, .271, and .058, respectively. The main change in the impact multipliers occurs for I^c and II.

The effects of changes in k_1 and k_2 on GNP are also much more powerful in Table VI compared with Table I. Column 2, which records the impacts of k_1, reports a decrease in GNP equal to 3.3 billion in Table VI compared with a decrease of .38 billion in Table I. The entry for GNP in column 3 of Table VI (the multiplier for k_2) is -1.45, compared with $-.34$ for the corresponding element in Table I.

There is one "inconsistency" in the impact multipliers with this direct monetary channel. In column 2 of Table VI the impacts of k_1 on interest rates are negative rather than positive. As seen from Table I, the signs for the multipliers of k_1 and k_2 ought to be the same, and both are opposite the signs of the multipliers recorded for Z. This is not true of the multipliers on interest rates in column 2 of Table VI. From a simple theoretical standpoint also (such as the simple IS-LM model), increases in k_1 should raise open market rates because it reduces the supply of money. The explanation for the negative impact of k_1 on rates is quite simple, however. It was suggested (in the section giving a general description of policy multipliers on interest rates) that if income increases to a large extent, then an expansionary monetary policy may reduce interest rates initially but that over a longer time period, rates may have the opposite sign. In column 2 of Table VI the impact of k_1 on Y is extremely large (especially compared with the multiplier for k_2). The large increase in Y and its effect on the Z market seems to require a decrease in i_{TB} (and therefore, other rates) to restore equilibrium. To test this hypothesis, the coefficient of k_1 in Equation 43 was reduced by one fifth, and the impact multipliers of k_1 were calculated.[21] The results appear in column 4 of Table VI under the heading (k_1). As can be seen, the multiplier on Y in column 4 is substantially reduced, and the impacts of k_1 on interest rates are now positive.

The experiments described in this section indicate that if a model takes account of the "availability effect" of monetary policy, producing a more direct monetary channel, the magnitude of the impact of policy on GNP is increased. It has also been shown that this kind of model can

---

[21] Equation 43 was linearized at fourth quarter values of 1965 before the reduced form equations were calculated. The coefficient of k_1 was the value of DD^* in that quarter. The reduction in the coefficient of k_1 was arbitrary. It was made to conform with the coefficient of k_2.

(though need not, as is evidenced by Ando and Goldfeld) generate unexpected results for monetary policy. These inconventional results persuaded us to await a more refined clarification of the "availability effect" before incorporating it into our "basic" model.

"THINNESS" AND EFFICIENCY OF THE CAPITAL MARKETS

The market for a security is described as "thin" if a "large" change in price (interest rate) occurs when there is an exogenous change in supply or demand. For example, if an exogenous increase (decrease) in supply (demand) causes a large increase in the rate of interest, the market is called "thin." Exactly what is meant by "large" in this context, naturally, is a subjective matter. Clearly, if a one billion dollar reduction in demand causes the corporate bond rate to rise from 4 percent to 6 percent, the market is certainly "thin." If that same change in demand causes the corporate bond rate to rise from 4 percent to 4.10 percent, the market would certainly not be called "thin." Where one draws the line is not subject to a clear-cut answer.

In the context of our model it is possible to examine the impact multipliers of an exogenous change in corporate bond demand (CB^x), mortgage demand (M^x), and state-local bond supply ($\overline{SL}$).[22] These multipliers are recorded in columns four, three, and one of Table VII, respectively (ignore column two for now). An increase (decrease) of one billion in CB^x causes a decrease (increase) of 28 basis points in i_{CB}. An increase (decrease) of one billion in M^x causes a decrease (increase) of 42 basis points in i_M. Neither of these markets can be called "thin," although the mortgage market is not as resilient as the corporate bond market. Note that because the *ceteris paribus* conditions are not satisfied in real-world observations, it is incorrect to suggest that our results are unrealistic simply because actual changes in i_{CB} and i_M are usually less than those recorded here (and with larger transactions). Notice also that the effects of changes in M^x and CB^x occur on all of the endogenous variables of the model; that is, these two markets are completely integrated into the model; there is no segmentation of these markets.

The multipliers of state-local bond supply, on the other hand, imply that the state-local market is segmented from the rest of the model. A change in $\overline{SL}$ affects i_{SL}, GB^o, and SL^o only. Second, the state-local bond market is extremely thin; an increase of one billion in $\overline{SL}$ increases i_{SL} by 6.25 percentage points (625 basis points). This unrealistic degree of

---

[22] The multipliers of an exogenous change in state-local demand (SL^x) are exactly the same as those of $\overline{SL}$ except they are of opposite sign.

Table VII
Impact Multipliers to Test "Thinness" of Bond Markets

	SL	$\overline{(SL)}$	M^x	CB^x
GB^u			.020	.037
CB^u			$-.021$	$-.129$
M^u			$-.045$	.191
GB^c		$-.757$	.018	.012
M^c			.005	.001
SL^c		.757	$-.005$	$-.003$
GBS^c/GB^c			.000	.000
ER^c			$-.004$	$-.001$
B^c			.009	.002
GB^s			.012	.004
M^s			.004	.002
GB^l			.001	.000
CB^l			.162	$-.111$
M^l			$-.010$	.077
GB^o	-2.174	$-.527$	$-.010$	$-.006$
SL^o	1.000	.242	.004	.003
GB^p			.012	.072
CB^p			$-.137$	$-.759$
$\overline{CB}$			.004	.001
$\overline{M}$			.952	.270
DD^c			.101	.039
TD^c			$-.054$	$-.033$
D^u			.028	.008
D^s			.010	.006
CUR			.003	.000
L^c			.048	.013
I^c			.010	.003
II			.007	.002
RC			.137	.039
C			.161	.046
Y			.316	.089
Y^p			.243	.069
Y^d			.219	.062
TX			.024	.007
RR			.010	.004
i_{TB}			.078	.024
i_{GB}			.018	.006
i_{CB}			$-.024$	$-.276$
i_M			$-.416$	$-.118$
i_{SL}	6.246	1.512	.049	.023
i_{BL}			$-.099$	$-.028$
i_{TD}			.000	.004

"thinness" in the state-local market stems from the peculiar features of this market cited before (the second section of this chapter) in connection with the interest rate impacts of monetary policy. Accordingly, the impact multipliers of $\overline{SL}$ were recalculated under the conditions of increased substitutability between state-local bonds and Governments that were also used to generate Table III. These multipliers are recorded in column 2 of Table VII under the heading $(\overline{SL})$. As can be seen, the impact of a billion dollar increase in $\overline{SL}$ on i_{SL} is only 1.51 percentage points or one-fourth the size of the corresponding multiplier recorded in column one.

The concept of thinness as just described is closely related to efficiency in the capital markets. The capital markets are efficient if they induce investment funds to flow into the sectors of the economy that contain the most profitable investment opportunities. Because our model sets the demand for a security equal to supply (as an equilibrium condition) in each period, it is not possible for an increased demand for funds to invest (in response to higher profitability in one sector) to remain unsatisfied. An increased demand for funds by home builders will increase mortgage supply; this increased supply is set equal to demand by the market-clearing equation for mortgages. Our measure of efficiency, therefore, must be based on the "ease" with which an increased demand for funds is satisfied. The "ease" factor may be defined in terms of the change in the rates of interest needed to induce the transfer of funds from one use to another. This concept of efficiency is linked closely with the operational efficiency of the capital markets in contrast with the term *efficiency* as used in the Pareto optimal sense.

From the multipliers in Table VII it is possible to conclude that the corporate bond market and the mortgage market are relatively efficient. A judgment regarding efficiency in the state-local bond must be reserved pending a more comprehensive analysis of that market. It is possible to conclude, however, that increased substitutability between securities will increase the efficiency of the capital markets (compare columns one and two of Table VII). Note that this is true only if it is assumed that increased substitutability raises the sensitivity of demand to the own rate of interest.[23] Although this seems correct intuitively, it has yet to be demonstrated rigorously.[24]

---

[23] Recall that the experiment that generated column two of Table VII included a positive coefficient of $+500.0$ for i_{SL} in the SL^c demand equation.

[24] Note that the experiments recorded in Tables IV and V regarding the effect of changes in substitutability on the efficacy of monetary policy *do not* impose the condition that decreased substitutability reduces the responsiveness of demand to the own rate. In this sense they are less restrictive. Had this condition been imposed, those results would have been even more forceful.

Chapter 6

CONCLUSION

The model of the financial sector of the U.S. economy developed in this study produced a number of results, the highlights of which can be summarized as follows.

BEHAVIOR OF FINANCIAL INTERMEDIARIES

We have examined the investment behavior of six types of financial institutions, savings banks, commercial banks, savings and loan associations, life insurance companies, pension plans, and other insurance companies, from which the following general conclusions can be drawn. The demands for different categories of securities are sensitive to interest rate differentials. All intermediaries, with the exception of commercial banks and savings and loan associations, adjust their investment portfolios in response to changes in relative rates of interest. For commercial banks, relative deposit flows seem to be the important determinants of portfolio composition. The portfolios of savings and loans are determined solely by their desire to meet the shelter needs of the public; that is, mortgages are held almost exclusively.

The use of the stock adjustment principle in the specification of the security demand equations of the financial sector seems to have been a reasonable assumption. The speeds of adjustment implied by the equations are fairly quick, especially when contrasted with the works of

De Leeuw and Goldfeld.[1] Our findings indicate also that significant differences exist between the behavior of the various financial institutions. Legal prescriptions, institutional peculiarities, and the nature of the institutions' liabilities demonstrate quite strongly that disaggregation of security demand equations by type of intermediary is extremely important.[2]

SUBSTITUTABILITY AND COMPLEMENTARITY BETWEEN SECURITIES

The underlying risk relationships between different categories of securities are the basic factors that determine whether two securities will be substitutes for, or complementary with, each other. In particular, Governments and corporates, mortgages and corporates, and municipals and Governments are all substitutes for each other, whereas Governments and mortgages are complementary in demand.

MONETARY POLICY

After estimating the structural set of equations representing behavior in the financial and nonfinancial sectors of the U.S. economy, we calculated the reduced form of the model. The impact multipliers corresponding to reserve requirement changes, discount rate changes, and open market operations reveal the importance of substitute and complement relationships between Government bonds and private debt instruments for the efficacy of monetary policy.

CAPITAL MARKET EFFICIENCY AND "THINNESS" OF THE BOND MARKETS

The general conclusion is that the capital markets can induce funds to flow into different investment categories with rather moderate changes in the structure of capital market rates. With regard to the closely related question of "thinness" in the bond markets, it seems that a changed supply or demand for corporates and mortgages can take place without a major disturbance in these capital market yields.

[1] See [12] and [22].
[2] The failure to disaggregate might help explain the very long speeds of adjustment found by De Leeuw in [12].

Appendix A

INTEREST
ELASTICITIES
OF SECURITY
DEMANDS

In the text the substitute-complement relationships between securities were judged based on the signs and statistical significance of the interest rate variables in the security demand equations. The relative magnitudes of these relationships could not be ascertained because the degree of substitutability was not standardized for differences in scale. The elasticities and cross-elasticities of demand provide such a standardization. In Table VIII these elasticities are recorded for all interest-sensitive security demands by financial intermediaries. In the left-hand column each security is recorded, while in the top row the relevant interest rates are set forth at the head of each column. The first entry in column one, for example, means that the short-run elasticity of GB^u with respect to i_{GB} is .138. The long-run elasticity is recorded below the short-run figure and in parentheses; that is, for GB^u with respect to i_{GB}, the long-run elasticity is 1.648. In general, the long-run figures seem to indicate strong elasticities of substitution except for life insurance companies.

Table VIII
Elasticities of Security Demands by Financial Intermediaries

Elasticity of	With Respect to					
	i_{GB}	i_{CB}	i_M	i_{SL}	i_{TB}	i_{FHLB}
GB^u	.138 (1.648)	−.072 (−.861)				
CB^u	−.632 (−3.291)	.651 (3.393)				
M^u	.077 (.701)	−.141 (−1.280)	.053 (.487)			
GBS^c/GB^c	−.103 (−2.066)				.232 (4.646)	
GB^s	.506 (.900)					−.063 (−.113)
M^s						−.007 (−.023)
GB^p	.364 (1.362)	−.397 (−1.488)				
CB^p	−1.067 (−4.169)	.899 (3.368)				
GB^o	.248 (2.851)			−.076 (−.878)		
SL^o	−.103 (−2.957)			.029 (.826)		
GB^l	.032 (.178)					
CB^l	−.026 (−.321)	.058 (.714)	−.052 (−.636)			
M^l	.022 (.197)	−.034 (−.311)	.007 (.068)			

Appendix B

LIST OF VARIABLES AND EQUATIONS

In the following pages the endogenous variables, exogenous variables, and a condensed form of the structural equations of the "basic" model (without the coefficients of the seasonals) are presented.

ENDOGENOUS VARIABLES

GB^u	Government bonds of mutual savings banks (MSB)
CB^u	Corporate bonds of MSB
M^u	Mortgages of MSB
D^u	Deposits of MSB
GB^c	Government bonds of commercial banks (CB)
M^c	Mortgages of CB
SL^c	State-local bonds of CB
GBS^c/GB^c	Short-term Governments divided by GB^c of CB
ER^c	Excess reserves of CB
B^c	Borrowings from the "Fed" of CB
DD^c	Demand deposits of CB
TD^c	Time deposits of CB
GB^s	Government bonds of saving and loan associations (SLA)
M^s	Mortgages of SLA

D^s	Deposits of SLA
GB^l	Government bonds of life insurance companies (LIC)
CB^l	Corporate bonds of LIC
M^l	Mortgages of LIC
GB^o	Government bonds of "other" insurance companies (OIC)
SL^o	State-local bonds of OIC
GB^p	Government bonds of pension plans (PP)
CB^p	Corporate bonds of PP
$\overline{CB}$	Corporate bonds outstanding (supply)
$\overline{M}$	Mortgages outstanding (supply)
CUR	Currency held by the public
L^c	Loans (commercial and industrial) of CB
I^c	Investment by corporations
II	Inventory investment
RC	Residential construction
C	Consumption
Y	GNP
Y^p	Personal income
Y^d	Disposable income
TX	Personal income taxes
RR	Required reserves
i_{TB}	Treasury bill rate
i_{GB}	Long-term Government bond rate
i_{CB}	Corporate bond rate (BAA)
i_M	Mortgage rate (conventional)
i_{SL}	State-local bond rate
i_{BL}	Bank loan rate
i_{TD}	Commercial bank time deposit rate

EXOGENOUS VARIABLES (EXCEPT LAGGED DEPENDENT)

Z	Unborrowed reserves plus currency (Note: R^u in Equations 8 and 9 is $(Z - CUR)$ or unborrowed reserves)
k_1	Required reserves ratio on DD^c
k_2	Required reserves ratio on TD^c
i_D	Federal Reserve discount rate
i_{MTD}	Maximum time deposit rate
G	Government expenditure
i_{FHLB}	Federal Home Loan Bank borrowing rate
S_i	Seasonal dummy variables

$(D + T)^c{}_G$	Demand plus time deposits at CB by Federal and state-local governments
TXA^c	Tax accrual of CB
A^p	Assets of pension plans
$\Delta SPL/SPL$	Rate of change in stock price level
A^o	Assets of "other" insurance companies
$\Delta P/P$	Rate of change in the GNP deflator
A^l	Assets of life insurance companies (LIC)
L/V	Loan-to-value ratio on mortgages
CM^l	Commitments to mortgages by LIC
i_S	Interest rate on SLA shares
i_U	Interest rate on MSB deposits
RD	Retained earnings plus depreciation of corporations
P	GNP deflator
CU	Capacity utilization
MUO	Manufacturers unfilled orders
LA	Length of amortization on mortgages
ΔHH	Household formation
PRC/P_c	Rent component of consumer price index divided by consumer price index
CB^x	Exogenous corporate bond demand
M^x	Exogenous mortgage demand
SL^x	Exogenous state-local bond demand
$\overline{SL}$	State-local bond supply
β_1, β_2	Constants expressing the relationship between GNP and personal income (β_2 has been set at .77 for 1965)
α_1, α_2	Constants expressing the relationship between personal taxes and Y^p (α_2 has been set at .11 for 1965)
θ_1, θ_2	Constants reflecting the distribution of deposits by Federal and state-local governments between demand and time deposits

STRUCTURAL EQUATIONS OF THE MODEL

$$GB^u = 280.8\ i_{GB} - 116.0\ i_{CB} + .458\ \Delta D^u - .029\ D^u$$
$$(3.13) \qquad (1.73) \qquad (5.46) \qquad (4.60)$$
$$+ .916\ GB^u{}_{-1} + 82.9 + S_i$$
$$(22.0) \qquad (1.35)$$

$$R^2 = .99 \qquad SE/DV = .0095$$
$$SE = 69.3 \qquad DW = 1.92$$

(1)

$$CB^u = 456.2\ i_{CB} - 559.4\ i_{GB} + .009\ D^u$$
$$\qquad (3.54) \qquad\quad (3.00) \qquad\quad (1.46)$$
$$\qquad + .808\ CB^u_{-1} + 221.1 + S_i$$
$$\qquad\quad (9.76) \qquad\qquad (1.10)$$
$$\qquad R^2 = .826 \quad SE/DV = .052$$
$$\qquad SE = 164.6 \quad DW = 1.89$$

(2)

$$M^u/D^u = -.013\ (i_{CB} - i_M) + .009\ (i_{GB} - i_M)$$
$$\qquad\qquad (5.34) \qquad\qquad\quad (4.78)$$
$$\qquad + .89\ (M^u/D^u)_{-1} - .11\ (GB^u/D^u)_{-1}$$
$$\qquad\quad (25.7) \qquad\qquad\qquad (2.94)$$
$$\qquad + .103 + S_i$$
$$\qquad\quad (3.37)$$
$$\qquad R^2 = .99 \qquad SE/DV = .003$$
$$\qquad SE = .002 \qquad DW = 1.65$$

(3)

$$GB^c = .628\ DD^c + .675\ (D + T)^c_G - .946\ \Delta L^c$$
$$\qquad (2.70) \qquad\quad (4.61) \qquad\qquad\quad (4.75)$$
$$\qquad - .579\ DD^c_{-1} - .648\ (D + T)^c_{G-1}$$
$$\qquad\quad (2.97) \qquad\qquad (4.30)$$
$$\qquad + .936\ GB^c_{-1} - 1518.9 + S_i$$
$$\qquad\quad (14.4) \qquad\qquad (.15)$$
$$\qquad R^2 = .85 \qquad SE/DV = .021$$
$$\qquad SE = 1394.0 \qquad DW = 2.30$$

(4)

$$M^c = .014\ DD^c + .049\ TD^c + .123\ \Delta L^c$$
$$\qquad (.55) \qquad\quad (3.65) \qquad\quad (2.11)$$
$$\qquad + .873\ M^c_{-1} - 969.0 + S_i$$
$$\qquad\quad (18.9) \qquad\quad (.47)$$
$$\qquad R^2 = .99 \qquad SE/DV = .012$$
$$\qquad SE = 239.8 \quad DW = 1.85$$

(5)

$$SL^c = .077\ TD^c + .046\ (D + T)^c_{G-1} + .719\ SL^c_{-1}$$
$$\qquad (3.25) \qquad\quad (1.73) \qquad\qquad\qquad (8.05)$$
$$\qquad - 1237.1 + S_i$$
$$\qquad\quad (4.01)$$
$$\qquad R^2 = .99 \qquad\qquad SE/DV = .024$$
$$\qquad SE = 260.1 \qquad\quad DW = 2.01$$
$$\qquad\qquad\qquad\qquad RHO = .45$$

(6)

$$GBS^c/GB^c = .027\ i_{TB} - .009\ i_{GB} - .0003\ \Delta M^c + .006\ TXA^c$$
$$\quad(2.17)\qquad\quad(.45)\qquad\quad(2.19)\qquad\quad(1.86)$$
$$\quad + .95\ (GBS^c/GB^c)_{-1} - .051 + S_i$$
$$\quad(16.8)\qquad\qquad\qquad(1.40)$$
$$R^2 = .88\qquad SE/DV = .098$$
$$SE = .031\qquad DW = 1.41$$

(7)

$$ER^c = -52.0\ i_{TB} + .066\ \Delta R^u + .525\ ER^c_{-1} + 413.0 + S_i$$
$$\quad(2.71)\qquad\quad(1.93)\qquad\quad(3.58)\qquad\qquad(2.83)$$
$$R^2 = .80\qquad\qquad SE/DV = .101$$
$$SE = 53.0\qquad\qquad DW = 1.72$$

(8)

$$B^c = 102.0\ (i_{TB} - i_D) - .405\ \Delta R^u + .771\ B^c_{-1} + 368.0\ S_i$$
$$\quad(1.28)\qquad\qquad\qquad(5.01)\qquad\quad(13.5)\qquad\quad(6.24)$$
$$R^2 = .88\qquad\qquad SE/DV = .238$$
$$SE = 106.0\qquad\qquad DW = 2.27$$

(9)

$$GB^s = 632.3\ i_{GB} - 79.2\ i_{FHLB} + .031\ D^s + .440\ GB^s_{-1}$$
$$\quad(5.74)\qquad\quad(2.12)\qquad\qquad(4.76)\qquad\quad(3.90)$$
$$\quad - 1198.7 + S_i$$
$$\quad(4.98)$$
$$R^2 = .99\qquad\qquad SE/DV = .02$$
$$SE = 92.3\qquad\qquad DW = 1.67$$

(10)

$$M^s = -114.1\ i_{FHLB} + .380\ D^s + .639\ M^s_{-1} - 126.9 + S_i$$
$$\quad(.91)\qquad\qquad(4.39)\qquad\quad(7.30)\qquad\qquad(.23)$$
$$R^2 = .99\qquad\qquad SE/DV = .011$$
$$SE = 186.9\qquad\qquad DW = 1.55$$
$$RHO = .73$$

(11)

$$GB^l = 65.6\ i_{GB} - 1647.8\ (\Delta P/P) + .429\ \Delta A^l - .016\ A^l$$
$$\quad(.83)\qquad\qquad(2.72)\qquad\qquad\qquad(3.10)\qquad\quad(3.83)$$
$$\quad + .818\ GB^l_{-1} + 1968.7 + S_i$$
$$\quad(16.4)\qquad\qquad(2.73)$$
$$R^2 = .99\qquad\qquad SE/DV = .016$$
$$SE = 116.4\qquad\qquad DW = 1.67$$

(12)

$$CB^l = 583.9\ i_{CB} - 331.6\ i_{GB} - 438.3\ i_M - 433.1\ (\Delta P/P)$$
$$\quad(2.18)\qquad\qquad(1.69)\qquad\qquad(1.60)\qquad\quad(.64)$$
$$\quad + .034\ A^l + .919\ CB^l_{-1} + 1612.9 + S_i$$
$$\quad(1.59)\qquad\quad(15.0)\qquad\qquad(2.66)$$
$$R^2 = .99\qquad\qquad SE/DV = .003$$
$$SE = 129.3\qquad\qquad DW = 1.68$$

(13)

$$M^l = -292.5\ (i_{CB} - i_M) + 240.1\ (i_{GB} - i_M) - 61.7\ L/V$$
$$\quad\quad (1.26) \quad\quad\quad\quad (1.37) \quad\quad\quad\quad (1.68)$$
$$+ .059\ A^l + .541\ CM_{-2} + .891\ M^l_{-1} + 281.6$$
$$\quad (2.00) \quad\quad (3.17) \quad\quad\quad (15.3) \quad\quad\quad (1.42)$$
$$R^2 = .99 \quad\quad\quad\quad SE/DV = .005$$
$$SE = 181.1 \quad\quad\quad\quad DW = 2.37$$

(14)

$$GB^o = 394.7\ i_{GB} - 348.1\ i_{SL} + .102\ \Delta A^o - .014\ A^o$$
$$\quad\quad (4.16) \quad\quad (3.96) \quad\quad (2.89) \quad\quad (3.54)$$
$$+ .913\ GB^o_{-1} + 487.7 + S_i$$
$$\quad (15.9) \quad\quad\quad (1.22)$$
$$R^2 = .94 \quad\quad\quad\quad SE/DV = .01$$
$$SE = 59.2 \quad\quad\quad\quad DW = 1.64$$

(15)

$$SL^o/A^o = .004\ i_{SL} - .005\ i_{GB} - .021\ (\Delta SPL/SPL)$$
$$\quad\quad\quad (2.23) \quad\quad (2.45) \quad\quad\quad (3.77)$$
$$+ .965\ (SL^o/A^o)_{-1} + .017 + S_i$$
$$\quad (69.2) \quad\quad\quad\quad (6.46)$$
$$R^2 = .99 \quad\quad\quad\quad SE/DV = .009$$
$$SE = .002 \quad\quad\quad\quad DW = 1.05$$

(16)

$$GB^p = 295.1\ i_{GB} - 255.2\ i_{CB} + .003\ A^p + .733\ GB^p_{-1}$$
$$\quad\quad (2.52) \quad\quad (3.21) \quad\quad (1.10) \quad\quad (8.64)$$
$$+ 809.9 + S_i$$
$$\quad (2.68)$$
$$R^2 = .94 \quad\quad\quad\quad SE/DV = .033$$
$$SE = 96.8 \quad\quad\quad\quad DW = 2.09$$

(17)

$$CB^p/A^p = -.057\ i_{GB} + .038\ i_{CB} + .744\ (CB^p/A^p)_{-1}$$
$$\quad\quad\quad (2.30) \quad\quad (2.07) \quad\quad (6.54)$$
$$+ .141 + S_i$$
$$\quad (1.85)$$
$$R^2 = .88 \quad\quad\quad\quad SE/DV = .05$$
$$SE = .008 \quad\quad\quad\quad DW = 1.77$$
$$\quad\quad\quad\quad\quad\quad RHO = .66$$

(18)

$$\overline{CB} = .366\ I^c - .252\ RD_{-1} + .98\ \overline{CB}_{-1} + 1229.7 + S_i$$
$$\quad\quad (4.33) \quad\quad (4.12) \quad\quad\quad (126.7) \quad\quad (4.67)$$
$$R^2 = .99 \quad\quad\quad\quad SE/DV = .005$$
$$SE = 333.5 \quad\quad\quad\quad DW = 2.28$$

(19)

$$\Delta \overline{M} = -2287.7\ \Delta i_M + .009\ \Delta Y^d + .777\ \Delta HH$$
$$\qquad (2.55) \qquad\qquad (1.80) \qquad\qquad (.57)$$
$$\qquad + .820\ \Delta \overline{M}_{-1} + S_i$$
$$\qquad\ \ (8.73)$$
$$R^2 = .90 \qquad\quad SE/DV = .116$$
$$SE = 487.4 \qquad DW = 2.61$$

(20)

$$DD^c/Y = -.012\ i_{TB} - .019\ i_{TD} + .620\ (DD^c/Y)_{-1}$$
$$\qquad\quad\ \ (3.91) \qquad\ \ (3.05) \qquad\ \ (5.74)$$
$$\qquad + .540 + S_i$$
$$\qquad\ \ (3.34)$$
$$R^2 = .99 \qquad\quad SE/DV = .014$$
$$SE = .013 \qquad DW = 1.71$$

(21)

$$TD^c/Y = .020\ i_{TD} - .008\ i_{TB} - .774\ \Delta Y/Y_{-1}$$
$$\qquad\quad\ \ (3.02) \qquad\ \ (2.72) \qquad\ \ (6.38)$$
$$\qquad + .926\ (TD^c/Y)_{-1} + .046 + S_i$$
$$\qquad\ \ (18.5) \qquad\qquad\qquad (2.52)$$
$$R^2 = .99 \qquad\quad SE/DV = .018$$
$$SE = .011 \qquad DW = 2.15$$

(22)

$$D^u/Y = .006\ i_U - .005\ i_{GB} + .787\ (D^u/Y)_{-1} + .039 + S_i$$
$$\qquad\ \ (2.71) \qquad (2.13) \qquad\quad (10.7) \qquad\qquad (2.15)$$
$$R^2 = .92 \qquad\qquad SE/DV = .014$$
$$SE = .004 \qquad\qquad DW = 1.77$$

(23)

$$D^s = .051\ Y - 382.2\ i_{GB} - 773.2\ i_{TD} + 1590.0\ i_S$$
$$\qquad (1.93) \qquad (1.54) \qquad\ \ (3.04) \qquad\quad (4.16)$$
$$\qquad + .976\ D^s_{-1} - 5531.3 + S_i$$
$$\qquad\ \ (40.0) \qquad\quad (2.42)$$
$$R^2 = .99 \qquad\qquad SE/DV = .005$$
$$SE = 247.3 \qquad\quad DW = 1.89$$
$$\qquad\qquad\qquad\quad\ RHO = .15$$

(24)

$$CUR = -1916.0\ i_{GB} + .119\ Y + .283\ CUR_{-1} + 16659.0 + S_i$$
$$\qquad\quad (1.95) \qquad\qquad (3.55) \qquad (1.74) \qquad\qquad (2.06)$$
$$R^2 = .78 \qquad\qquad\quad SE/DV = .046$$
$$SE = 1539.8 \qquad\qquad DW = 2.13$$

(25)

$$\Delta L^c = .468\ \Delta II - 450.0\ \Delta i_{BL} + .544\ \Delta L^c_{-1}$$
$$\qquad\ \ (6.00) \qquad\quad (1.10) \qquad\quad (6.75)$$
$$R^2 = .78 \qquad\quad DW = 1.98$$
$$SE = 406.0$$

(26)

$$I^c/P = \begin{array}{c} .013 \\ (2.31) \end{array} Y/P + \begin{array}{c} .133 \\ (4.28) \end{array} \Delta L^c/P + \begin{array}{c} 18.8 \\ (3.14) \end{array} CU_{-1}$$

$$+ \begin{array}{c} .840 \\ (14.6) \end{array} (I^c/P)_{-1} - \begin{array}{c} 1907.2 \\ (2.74) \end{array} + S_i \tag{27}$$

$$R^2 = .98 \qquad SE/DV = .027$$
$$SE = 221.0 \qquad DW = 1.73$$

$$II/P = \begin{array}{c} .146 \\ (1.64) \end{array} \Delta L^c/P + \begin{array}{c} 122.1 \\ (3.45) \end{array} \Delta MUO_{-1} + \begin{array}{c} .302 \\ (2.75) \end{array} (II/P)_{-1}$$

$$- \begin{array}{c} 48.97 \\ (.18) \end{array} + S_i \tag{28}$$

$$R^2 = .71 \qquad SE/DV = .917$$
$$SE = 612.0 \qquad DW = 2.18$$

$$RC/P = \begin{array}{c} -294.5 \\ (1.77) \end{array} i_M + \begin{array}{c} 92.8 \\ (2.82) \end{array} LA + \begin{array}{c} .692 \\ (1.13) \end{array} \Delta HH$$

$$+ \begin{array}{c} 38.3 \\ (1.01) \end{array} PRC/P_C + \begin{array}{c} .688 \\ (7.70) \end{array} (RC/P)_{-1} - \begin{array}{c} 2927.7 \\ (.64) \end{array} + S_i \tag{29}$$

$$R^2 = .92 \qquad SE/DV = .044$$
$$SE = 252.3 \qquad DW = 1.47$$

$$C/P = \begin{array}{c} .738 \\ (5.19) \end{array} Y^d/P + \begin{array}{c} .223 \\ (1.42) \end{array} (C/P)_{-1} + \begin{array}{c} 4846.0 \\ (4.45) \end{array} + S_i$$

$$R^2 = .99 \qquad SE/DV = .011 \tag{30}$$
$$SE = 888.4 \qquad DW = 1.91$$

$$Y = C + I^c + II + RC + G \tag{31}$$

$$Y^p = \beta_1 + \beta_2 Y \tag{32}$$

$$Y^d = Y^p - TX \tag{33}$$

$$TX = \alpha_1 + \alpha_2 Y^p \tag{34}$$

$$RR = k_1 DD^c + k_2 TD^c + (\theta_1 k_1)(\theta_2 k_2)(D + T)^c{}_G \tag{35}$$

$$Z = RR + ER^c - B^c + CUR \tag{36}$$

$$i_{GB} = \begin{array}{c} .124 \\ \end{array} + \begin{array}{c} .949 \\ (23.5) \end{array} i_{GB-1} + \begin{array}{c} .234 \\ (7.67) \end{array} i_{TB} - \begin{array}{c} .206 \\ (7.00) \end{array} i_{TB-1}$$

$$R^2 = .977 \qquad DW = 2.02 \tag{37}$$
$$SE = .094$$

$$CB^u + CB^l + CB^p + CB^x = \overline{CB} \tag{38}$$

$$M^u + M^s + M^c + M^l + M^x = \overline{M} \tag{39}$$

$$SL^c + SL^o + SL^x = \overline{SL} \tag{40}$$

$$
\begin{aligned}
i_{BL} = \ &.275 \ i_M + \ .191 \ i_{TB} + \ .568 \ i_{BL-1} - \ .138 \ + S_i \\
&(2.16) \qquad (7.51) \qquad\ \ (5.46) \qquad\qquad (.42) \\
&R^2 = .96 \qquad\qquad SE/DV = .026 \\
&SE = .116 \qquad\qquad DW = 1.70
\end{aligned}
\tag{41}
$$

$$
\begin{aligned}
i_{TD} = \ &-.362 + .0158 \, [L^c/(DD + TD)] + .016 \ i_{CB} \\
&+ .463 \ i_{MTD} - .360 \ i_{MTD-1} + .869 \ i_{TD-1} \\
&R^2 = .975 \qquad\qquad DW = 2.55 \quad \text{(for annual eq.)} \\
&SE = .028
\end{aligned}
\tag{42}
$$

Appendix C

MULTIPLIERS WITH IMPOSITION OF BALANCE SHEET IDENTITIES

In the section "Specification of the Demand Equations" in Chapter 2, it was noted that balance sheet identities for each intermediary setting total portfolio assets equal to total liabilities are not included in our model. These identities, together with the residual elements in the various portfolios, were dropped from the explicit structural model. Although this is a legitimate procedure, it was noted throughout Chapter 3 that the various portfolio demand equations of each intermediary still had to satisfy certain a priori consistency checks such as those set forth by Brainard and Tobin. It was also noted that failure to include the balance sheet identity implicitly assumes that the residual elements in each institution's portfolio absorbs any discrepancy between changes in assets and liabilities.

The impact multipliers in Tables I and I.D reveal that changes in the liabilities of commercial banks, savings banks, and savings and loan associations due to any given policy change do not equal the sum of the change in assets of each institution. (The equilibrium multipliers of Table II should not be looked at for this purpose because, as noted in Chapter 5, there are conceptual problems in their interpretation.) Presumably, the items in the balance sheets of these institutions that do not appear as endogenous variables in the model make up the difference. Note that because the liabilities of the other institutions (for example, life insurance companies) in our model are exogenous, this "inconsistency" in the multi-pliers is only explicit for banks and savings and loan associations.

The problem with the impact multipliers is particularly acute for commercial banks because even the cash items in their balance sheets were included as endogenous variables. For savings banks and savings and loan associations it might be argued that cash items change in the short run to balance the portfolio. Given the recent interest in this prob-lem of financial-model building, it was decided to re-estimate the reduced form after the following three identities were imposed (where X^u, X^s, and X^c are the exogenous assets of each intermediary).

$$GB^u + CB^u + M^u + X^u = D^u \tag{i}$$
$$GB^s + M^s + X^s = D^s \tag{ii}$$
$$GB^c + SL^c + M^c + ER^c + L^c + RR + X^c$$
$$= DD^c + TD^c + B^c + (D + T)^c{}_G \tag{iii}$$

Imposing these three equations on the model requires that three others be dropped. The equations to be dropped should be for the assets whose demands are most easily represented as a residual. It is very difficult to choose which structural equations currently in the model are really demand equations for an asset that is a residual. A fairly good case might be made for Government bond demand, although arguments for the residual nature of any of the other demands could also be made. Equations i, ii, and iii just listed were, in fact, substituted for the demand equations for GB^u, GB^s, and GB^c, and the impact multipliers were recalculated. The results were that the impacts on all of the endogenous variables, including interest rates, were unchanged except for the effects on GB^u, GB^s, and GB^c. This, of course, is not very surprising because the Government bond demand equations play no role in market interactions. They form an independent subset of the structural model. The interest rate on Govern-ments is "determined" by a term structure relationship rather than a market equilibrium condition. Had there been a market-clearing equation for Governments, the multipliers on the rest of the model would have certainly changed.

This exercise was mentioned only to demonstrate that within the context of our model the balance sheet constraint can be imposed without substantially changing the characteristics of the model. Obviously, if the demand equations for mortgages of each of these institutions were dropped, the resulting impact multipliers would have been different. The fact that the sectors of the model are not fully interrelated implies that, unlike the basic Walrasian system, it does make a difference which equation(s) is (are) dropped. Given the appended nature of the Government bond demand equations, however, the choice of dropping those relationships can be given additional justification.

One further comment is in order regarding the fact that the impact multipliers in a model change depending upon which equation(s) is (are) dropped. As was just mentioned, in a theoretical general equilibrium model Walras' law shows that any equation can be dropped and the solution to the system remains unchanged. This is not true in empirical econometric models for a number of reasons. First, most econometric models do not have (for practical reasons) all the equations of the general equilibrium model explicitly included in the calculation of the reduced form (as is true of our model). Second, in empirical models there are many "zeros" in the matrix of the coefficients of the endogenous variables. In a general Walrasian system all of the markets are totally interrelated and no explicit zeros appear. The point being made is that frequently there is only one explicit link between two markets. For example, empirically one usually finds only one or two interest rates in the money demand function, whereas theoretically there is a vector of all rates included in the money demand function. These factors make the calculated impact multipliers sensitive to slight changes in specification, especially where market interdependence is altered.

One example of drastic changes in multipliers can be given within the context of our model. In the basic structural system without any balance sheet constraints three equations had to be dropped corresponding to the three interest rates legally set equal to zero. In the trial investigations, other equations besides those that were finally dropped were also eliminated, and the respective reduced forms were recalculated. When the equations for ER^c or B^c were dropped in these initial experiments, the impacts of monetary policy (changes in Z, k_1, or k_2) on all of the endogenous variables (except ER^c or B^c) were zero. The reason is quite obvious. A change in Z, k_1, or k_2 produced disequilibrium in the market for "high-powered money." When one of the components of the demand for high-powered money (either ER^c or B^c) was looked upon as a residual, the disequilibrium in that market did not spill over to the rest of the system. In other words, the link between monetary policy and the rest of the model was broken. All effects of (say) open market operations were absorbed by changes in either excess reserves or borrowings (depending upon which structural equation was dropped). Had the balance sheet identity been imposed on commercial banks, however, the linkage between monetary policy and the rest of the model would not have been eliminated. This demonstrates quite vividly the sensistivity of econometric models that are not "fully specified" to slight changes in structural specification.

Appendix D

DESCRIPTION
OF THE DATA

ASSETS AND LIABILITIES OF
FINANCIAL INTERMEDIARIES

Unless otherwise indicated, all assets (for example, security holdings) and liabilities (for example, deposits) of financial institutions are taken from the *Flow of Funds Accounts, Seasonally Unadjusted*. This set of data is available from the Board of Governors of the Federal Reserve System. The raw data are in the form of quarterly flows and annual levels. All the data are in millions of dollars. We have used the quarterly flows in the form of quarter-to-quarter changes. Quarterly levels are derived by cumulating the flows during the year and adding this to the previous year's annual level. The constructed quarterly levels are forced into correspondence with the annual levels given in the F/F data. Unless we specify differently, all series used begin in the first quarter of 1953 and end in the fourth quarter of 1965. The variables presented below are what were used in asset or liability categories of the financial intermediaries, but were not taken from the F/F data, or were modified prior to their inclusion in our model.

> *Excess Reserves of Commercial Banks:* This series is taken from the *Federal Reserve Bulletin*, 1953–1965. The data are for the last month of the quarter.
>
> *Borrowings of Commercial Banks:* This series is taken from the *Federal*

Reserve Bulletin, 1953–1965. The data are for the last month of the quarter.

Unborrowed Reserves: This variable is defined as total reserves minus borrowed reserves. The precise construction of this variable and how it accounts for reserve requirement changes are explained in the July 1963 issue of the *Federal Reserve Bulletin.* The data from 1963 through 1965 were made available by the research department of the Federal Reserve Bank of New York. The data are for the last month of the quarter.

Commitments of Mortgages by Life Insurance Companies: The Life Insurance Association of America provided this set of data. The data are for the last month of the quarter, from 1953 through 1965.

FINANCIAL ASSETS

There is one financial asset in our system that is not a liability of private financial intermediaries and that was not, therefore, included under the first set of data discussed.

Currency: This includes currency outside the Treasury, the Federal Reserve System, and the vaults of all commercial banks. The data are for the last month of the quarter. The source is the *Federal Reserve Bulletin.*

INTEREST RATES

The interest rate variables were measured in percentages; that is, an interest rate of 2 percent is written as 2.00. Unless otherwise indicated, the data are from the *Federal Reserve Bulletin* and are for the last month of the quarter.

Treasury Bill Rate: The market yield on three-month bills.

Government Bond Rate: The rate on Government bonds above ten years to maturity. The series includes bonds as follows: beginning April, 1953, fully taxable marketable bonds due or callable in ten years or more; from April 1952, through March 1953, fully taxable marketable bonds due or first callable after twelve years; prior thereto, bonds due or callable after fifteen years.

Corporate Bond Rate: The data used were from the series prepared by Moody's Investors Service on BAA corporate bonds.

Mortgage Rate: Until 1956 the yield on conventional mortgages, as reported in [33] was used. The Division of Research and Statistics of the Federal Housing Authority has compiled a similar series since 1956 that we have used, called the yield on conventional first mortgages.

State-Local Bond Rate: The yield on fifteen high-grade municipals (Standard and Poor's average).

Bank Loan Rate: The data are an average of bank rates on short-term business loans in nineteen large cities. The rate is for loans that are above $200,000.

Time Deposit Rate: The annual series is reported in the Annual Reports of the Federal Deposit Insurance Corporation. The quarterly interpolation used to create the series used here is described in [13].

Rate on Mutual Savings Bank Deposits: The annual series was taken from the balance sheet reports of savings banks. A simple linear interpolation was used to construct the quarterly series.

Rate on Savings and Loan Shares: The annual series was taken from the balance sheet reports of savings associations. A linear interpolation was used to create the quarterly series.

Stock Price Average: The series used is Standard and Poor's average of five hundred common stocks.

Discount Rate: The rate as of the last day in the quarter.

Maximum Time Deposit Rate: The rate as of the last day in the quarter.

Federal Home Loan Bank Rate: A simple average of the rates charged by the various Federal Home Loan Banks. The data were provided by the Federal Home Loan Bank Board.

NATIONAL INCOME VARIABLES

All variables are in millions of dollars, expressed at quarterly rates, and are taken from the *Flow of Funds Accounts, Seasonally Unadjusted.*

Miscellaneous Variables

Capacity Utilization: The series used was taken from the *Federal Reserve Bulletin.*

Manufacturers Unfilled Orders: The data (seasonally unadjusted in millions of dollars) are for the last month of the quarter and were taken from *U.S. Business Statistics* and the *Survey of Current Business.*

Loan-to-Value Ratio on Mortgages: The data on conventional mortgages were used. The Division of Research of the FHA provided the data.

Length of Amortization on Mortgages: The data on conventional mortgages were used. The Division of Research of the FHA provided the data.

Household Formation: A quarterly (linear) interpolation of the annual estimate of the number of households by the Census Bureau in their current population reports.

Rent Component of Consumer Price Index: Various issues of the *Survey of Current Business.*

Consumer Price Index: Various issues of the *Survey of Current Business.*

GNP Deflator: Various issues of the *Survey of Current Business.*

BIBLIOGRAPHY

1. American Bankers Association, *The Commercial Banking Industry*, Englewood Cliffs, N.J., Prentice-Hall, Inc., 1962.

2. American Mutual Insurance Alliance *et. al.*, *Property and Casualty Insurance Companies: Their Role as Financial Intermediaries*, Englewood Cliffs, N.J., Prentice-Hall, Inc., 1962.

3. Anderson, W. H. L., *Corporate Finance and Fixed Investment: An Econometric Study*, Boston, Division of Research, Graduate School of Business Administration, Harvard University, 1964.

4. Ando, Albert, and S. M. Goldfeld, "An Econometric Model for Stabilization Policies" in *Studies in Economic Stabilization* (Ando, Brown, and Friedlaender, eds.), Brookings Institution, Washington, D.C., 1968.

5. Baumol, William J., "The Transactions Demand for Cash, An Inventory Theoretical Approach," *Quarterly Journal of Economics*, 1952.

6. Baxter, Nevins, *The Commercial-Paper Market*, Princeton, N.J., Econometric Research Program, 1964.

7. Brainard, W. C., and J. Tobin, "Pitfalls in Financial Model Building," *American Economic Review*, May 1968, pp. 99–122.

8. Commission on Money and Credit, *Fiscal and Debt Management Policies*, Englewood Cliffs, N.J., Prentice-Hall, Inc., 1963.

9. ———, *Impacts of Monetary Policy*, Englewood Cliffs, N.J., Prentice-Hall, Inc., 1963.

10. ———, *Private Capital Markets*, Englewood Cliffs, N.J., Prentice-Hall, Inc., 1964.

11. ———, *Stabilization Policies*, Englewood Cliffs, N.J., Prentice-Hall, Inc., 1963.

12. De Leeuw, Frank, "A Model of Financial Behavior" in *Brookings Quarterly Econometric Model of the United States*, Skokie, Ill., Rand McNally & Company, 1965, Chapter 13.

13. ———, "Financial Markets in Business Cycles: A Simulation Study," *American Economic Review*, May 1964, pp. 309–323.

14. ———, and Edward Gramlich, "The Federal Reserve—MIT Econometric Model," *Federal Reserve Bulletin*, January 1968.

15. Duesenberry, James, Gary Fromm, Lawrence Klein, and Edwin Kuh, *Brookings Quarterly Econometric Model of the United States*, Skokie, Ill., Rand McNally & Company, 1965.

16. Fand, David, "Financial Regulation and the Allocative Efficiency of Our Capital Markets," *National Banking Review*, September 1965.

17. Feige, Edgar L., *The Demand for Liquid Assets: A Temporal Cross-Section Analysis*, Englewood Cliffs, N.J., Prentice-Hall, Inc., 1964.

18. Fisher, Franklin M., "The Choice of Instrumental Variables in the Estimation of Economy-wide Econometric Models," *International Economic Review*, Volume 6, No. 3, pp. 245–275.

19. Friedman, Milton, "The Role of Monetary Policy," *American Economic Review*, March 1968.

20. Goldberger, Arthur S., *Econometric Theory*, New York, John Wiley & Sons, Inc., 1964.

21. ———, *Impact Multipliers and Dynamic Properties of the Klein-Goldberger Model*, Amsterdam, North-Holland Publishing Co., 1959.

22. Goldfeld, Stephen M., *Commercial Bank Behavior and Economic Activity: A Structural Study of Monetary Policy in Postwar United States*, Amsterdam, North-Holland Publishing Co., 1966.

23. ———, and E. J. Kane, "The Determinants of Member Bank Borrowing," *Journal of Finance*, September 1966.

24. Hamburger, Michael J., "Household Demand for Financial Assets," *Econometrica*, January 1968.

25. ――――, and Cynthia Latta, "The Term Structure of Interest Rates: Additional Evidence," *Journal of Money, Credit and Banking*, February 1969.

26. Haywood, Charles F., *The Pledging of Bank Assets*, Chicago, Ill., Association of Reserve City Bankers, 1967.

27. Hendershott, Patric, "Recent Development of the Financial Sector of Econometric Models," *Journal of Finance*, March 1968.

28. Henderson, James, and Richard Quandt, *Microeconomic Theory*, New York, McGraw-Hill, Inc., 1958.

29. Hester, Donald, "A Model of Portfolio Behavior Applied to Mutual Savings Banks," Cowles Foundation, New Haven, Conn., Yale University.

30. Johnston, J., *Econometric Methods*, New York, McGraw-Hill, Inc., 1963.

31. Keare, Douglas, and William L. Silber, "The Monetary Effect of Long-Term Debt Finance," *American Economic Review*, June 1965.

32. Kendall, Leon T., *The Savings and Loan Business: Its Purposes, Functions, and Economic Justification*, Englewood Cliffs, N.J., Prentice-Hall, Inc., 1962.

33. Klaman, Saul, *The Postwar Residential Mortgage Market*, Princeton, N.J., Princeton University Press, for the National Bureau of Economic Research, 1961.

34. Klein, Lawrence, *An Introduction to Econometrics*, Englewood Cliffs, N.J., Prentice-Hall, Inc., 1962.

35. Kuenne, Robert, *The Theory of General Economic Equilibrium*, Princeton, N.J., Princeton University Press, 1963.

36. Levy, Michael, *Cycles in Government Securities, II, Determinants of Changes in Ownership*, New York, National Industrial Conference Board, 1965.

37. Life Insurance Association of America, *Life Insurance Companies as Financial Institutions*, Englewood Cliffs, N.J., Prentice-Hall, Inc., 1962.

38. Malkiel, Burton G., "Expectations, Bond Prices and the Term Structure of Interest Rates," *Quarterly Journal of Economics*, May 1962, pp. 197–218.

39. Modigliani, Franco, and Merton Miller, "Dividend Policy, Growth and Valuation of Shares," *Journal of Business*, October 1961, pp. 411–433.

40. National Association of Mutual Savings Banks, *Mutual Savings Banking: Basic Characteristics and Role in the National Economy*, Englewood Cliffs, N.J., Prentice-Hall, Inc., 1962.

41. Polakoff, M. E., "Federal Reserve Discount Policy and Its Critics," in *Banking and Monetary Studies*, (Deane Carson, ed.), Homewood, Ill., Richard D. Irwin, Inc., 1963.

42. ———, and W. L. Silber, "Reluctance and Member Bank Borrowing: Additional Evidence," *Journal of Finance*, March 1967.

43. Renshaw, Edward, "Portfolio Balance Models in Perspective," *Journal of Financial and Quantitative Analysis*, June 1967.

44. Robinson, Roland, *Money and Capital Markets*, New York, McGraw-Hill, Inc., 1964.

45. ———, *Postwar Market for State and Local Government Securities*, Princeton, N.J., Princeton University Press, 1960.

46. ———, *The Management of Bank Funds*, New York, McGraw-Hill, Inc., 1962.

47. Silber, William L., "An Econometric Model of the Mortgage Market," in *Cyclical and Growth Problems Facing the Savings and Loan Industry* (A. W. Sametz, ed.), Bulletin No. 46–47, Institute of Finance, New York University.

48. ———, "Liquidity Premium Theory: Some Observations," *Kyklos*, No. I, 1969.

49. ———, "Open Market Rates and Regulation Q," *National Banking Review*, March 1967.

50. ———, "Portfolio Substitutability, Regulations, and Monetary Policy," *Quarterly Journal of Economics*, May 1969.

51. Tucker, Donald, "Income Adjustment to Money-Supply Changes," *American Economic Review*, June 1966.

52. Wold, H., and L. Jureen, *Demand Analysis*, New York, John Wiley & Sons, Inc., 1953.

53. Wood, John, *An Econometric Model of the Term Structure of Interest Rates*, an unpublished Ph.D. dissertation, Purdue University, 1964.

INDEX